YOU'RE NOT THE BOSS OF ME...
I AM!

YOU'RE NOT THE BOSS OF ME...
I AM!

SECRETS OF AN ENTREPRENEUR
10 LESSONS LEARNED ON MY JOURNEY TO
PERSONAL AND FINANCIAL FREEDOM

DEANNA HODGES, MBA, MIB

"The Woman on Top series book You're Not the Boss of Me... I AM! Secrets of an Entrepreneur. 10 Lessons Learned on My Journey to Personal and Financial Freedom is packed with valuable lessons that are vital to the success of any business Deanna Hodges has learned these lessons over many years of building a business from the ground up. This book is a must-read from entrepreneurs of all stages."

Kevin Harrington,
Original Shark on Shark Tank,
Founder of As Seen on TV and
Inventor of the Infomercial.

"I have been blessed to have dual careers in the beauty industry and in the musicl entertainment industry which taught me the importance of always leveraging your current career and experience to set up or your next career, I have a 'VISION' and if you do as well you must create your own path by nurturing your entrepreneurial spirit and laying a strong foundation on which you can build your business. Part of my nurturing and insight came from Deanna Hodges. Deanna showed me up close the necessary work needed infrastrructure for my business to run successfully.

It won't be easy however it does become easier with the right guidance. 'You Are Not the Boss of me...I AM!' will help you get started building your dream."

Adrian Anderson,
Beauty Entrepreneur and Former
member of Grammy nominated
singing group Trin-i-tee 5:7.

CONTENTS

Acknowledgments xiv
Introduction xvi
Personal Message From The Author xviii
Getting Started 1
Building A Team 5
The Effective Leader 17
Run Your Business As If You Are Broke 21
Do What You Do Best 31
Know Your Customer And Your Market 37
Don't Reinvent The Wheel 45
Handle Your Business 51
Conviction 57
Giving Back 61
Know Your Story And How It Ends 67
Summary And Conclusion 71
Quick Review And Bite-Size Wisdom 75
Tools And Resources 79
About The Author.. XI
Other Books By Deanna Hodges XVI
Final Thought XVIII

I'm not hungry for success.

I am only hungry for good work, and that is how it is with most superstars.
Every day I tell myself how fortunate I am to be where I am.
- Akshay Kumar

Acknowledgements

My father gave me the greatest gift anyone could give another person, he believed in me

    - Jim Valvano

This book has been a labor of love for me and a journey across many years. Over the years I have worked with and crossed paths with many who have contributed to my success and the knowledge that I share with you in this book.

I must express my gratitude and love to the following people:

First and foremost, I have to give the biggest thanks of all to my dad, Joseph Edwin Hodges. He was the best boss I could have ever asked for. An extremely hard-working entrepreneur and a great man, he taught me the most important skills of all, work ethic and compassion and kindness for my employees. I worked with my dad in his landscaping business from the time I was 5 years old until his death when I was just a teenager. He gave me the greatest gifts I could have ever asked for. These things have been vital to my success. I got up early every single Saturday morning to go to work with him- and it was not optional. It was just the way it was. I also worked with him many summers. He even helped me to start my first small business when I was just a child. My first customer was Mrs. Jolly, the mom of his business partner. She hired me to cut her yard for $5 per week. I had one other client and that was my first business and what ultimately led me to this exact point.

A huge heartfelt thanks to my family and my friends who have always been understanding and patient when I missed holidays and events because of work.

I also give a big thank you to all of the bosses (good and bad) over the years that have pushed me to be better or that have showed me what not to do if you want to have happy and inspired employees. In addition, I wish to think all of the employees and interns that I have had over the years who have taught me so much and made me see things through fresh eyes.

Thank you so much to the many wonderful business people and peers who allowed me to interview them for this book and share their wisdom with me which I am in turn sharing with you.

So much thanks and love to my dogs who are my kids. They have lain by my feet or by my side patiently while I wrote this book and they have comforted me when I have become so frustrated by my lack of focus. I love them more than I can say. Animals are a true blessing and they love you just the same regardless of your success or struggles.

And finally, but definitely not least, are the women who have come before me, fought the fight and paved the way so that I, and other women, may rise.

Introduction

Whatever the mind of man can conceive and believe, it can achieve.

- Napoleon Hill

This is a book for women who are new entrepreneurs and those who want to be entrepreneurs. It doesn't matter if you are a seasoned executive stepping out on your own or someone entering the business world for the first time or someone in between. Let me start by saying that there is no big "secret" to building a strong successful business and there is no fail- proof blueprint either. There are things that you should keep in mind that will help you to become a better entrepreneur and this book will help you see some of these things upfront and hopefully they will save you valuable time and money.

These are lessons that many people, myself included, have spent years and tens or hundreds of thousands of dollars (and even more) learning. Lessons are extremely expensive and I would like to share some of mine with you here in hopes that it may make your journey smoother.

Unless you are independently wealthy or have big financial backing, just know that you will need to check your ego when you start a business. There is no place for ego or pride in the beginning and absolutely no reason for it. You need to humble yourself if you have not already done so or you risk getting in your own way and alienating everyone around you. You will work many long hours, many weekends and many holidays. Your business will become your life and all encompassing. You will do things that other people used to do for you like take out the trash and vacuum and do the filing and handle accounts payable and manage sales and so on and so on. You are not too good or too important to handle any task, however trivial, in the beginning. There is also an added perk of doing all of these things. You will learn your business inside and out and when you are able to start hiring staff, you will understand everything that they will be doing as well as how long it should take them to do it. I know this sounds a bit "big brotherish" but I have had many instances where I had employees tell me that it took 3 hours to do a task that I know should take less than 1 hour for even the most inexperienced person. Do not let your employees run you or run over you. Know your business!

If you truly want to be an entrepreneur and be the master of your own destiny, you must be willing to sacrifice it all and live like many people won't so that you can eventually live like most people cannot. You have to be willing to give up the excess in your life and sacrifice it all for your business if you wish to be successful. I know this sounds scary and daunting and downright unappealing but it is not as bad as you think. As you build and grow your business, the outside noise will fade away and you will feed on your own passion and ambition and you will love it. I would be willing to bet that you don't even miss most of it because you are so busy building your business and so invigorated by each success and milestone that the trappings of life almost seem insignificant, almost invisible. Some of those other things won't seem to matter as much after all.

This book is a compilation of incredibly expensive and even painful lessons that I have learned over the years. It is a guide to help you lay a solid foundation so that you can build a strong business. Laying a strong foundation will help give you a good chance of survival and will help you succeed as an entrepreneur. You will eventually learn these lessons whether it is from this book, from a mentor or through trial and error.

Personal Message from the Author

Breathe. Let go. And remind yourself that this very moment is the only one you know you have for sure

   -Oprah Winfrey

Entrepreneurs and business people do all kinds of things to clear their mind and open their mind to brainstorm and strategize. Me, I drive in silence, walk at the beach or ride my bike. Others run or meditate or any number of things to help find focus and clear out the noise. Find out what feeds your creative mind and do it regularly. Your mind is the single most valuable thing that you have. It is your creation machine and strategy maker and so many other things. It is the essence of your being.

It dawned on me this morning as I was taking an early morning bike ride near my home in Southern California that my bike ride was much like my business journey – and much like life in general. As I started my ride it was exceptionally cold and the wind was blowing against me. I was peddling hard but feeling like I was getting nowhere. My legs were burning and starting to feel like rubber bands. I wondered how long I could pedal and how far I could go before I had to stop. I knew there was a goal of where I wanted to get to so I said, "No matter what, I will get there. Regardless of how long it takes or how uncomfortable I am I will get there."

On the way there were challenges and many bumps in the road. On this particular day, my shoestring came untied and got caught in the chain, which caused a detour and an unexpected stop on my journey. It also caused a few bruises. In some places the path was smooth and in others it was very bumpy, rugged and uphill.

I encountered many people along the way, some aware of their surroundings and some not so much. When you are riding a bike and there are people around you on foot and some of them have small children and animals, you have to be incredible aware of not only yourself but aware of them as well. Distractions are everywhere.

Being unaware can certainly ruin someone's day. It always amazes me how many people go through life completely unaware and as in my bicycle ride, they just walk out in front of you without looking or even considering that there may be someone coming. This is how it is with many entrepreneurs and their businesses. They start a business without a plan and they wander aimlessly. They never lead or build with intention. They start with nothing but a dream or an idea. Don't get me wrong, the dream is so very important. After all, it is why you started a business in the first place. The dream is the seed from which your business grows. The dream can only take you so far without proper planning and vision. Throughout your journey you must be exceedingly aware of your environment. Execution Is key to building and sustaining your business.

When I finally reached that ever important point that I wanted to reach, I felt a tremendous sense of accomplishment. It is this way in my business as well as with all of the different milestones though out life. It is all a series of mini successes and accomplishments and failures and lessons. All of these accomplishments and milestones and lessons form the foundation of your business and determines how you will run your business and guide it through the good times and the bad. Use your lessons and experiences to grow yourself and your business. If you fail, fail up and do not lose the lesson. Failure is nothing to be ashamed of. It will bring you the best lessons and insight that you could ever get, that is if you are aware and present.

Also, on your path to building a successful business, just as I did with my bicycle ride, you may have to detour and change course quickly due to unexpected occurrences or changes in your customer, your industry, your market, the economy, political changes or even changes in your strategy overall. Sometimes these changes must be made quickly and you must react without much notice just as I had to do with my shoestring in the chain. There was no warning and I had no time to think about it or plan or do anything at all except react. These types of decisions have to be made right then and there based on the situation that is occurring at that exact moment. This is when it is more important than ever to truly understand your customer, your market and your business goals.

On the way back, after I had reached the point that I wanted to reach,

I turned to head back the way I had come. This time I had the wind at my back pushing me forward. But even with the wind at my back there were still portions of the path that were bumpy, uphill and challenging. I still had to be very aware of my surroundings and be able to change course at a moment's notice. Even when I was riding with the wind at my back and able to coast, I could never fully let my guard down or stop pushing forward. It is the same in business. You can never truly let your guard down until you completely step away from your business, hopefully because you sold it for a large amount of money or passed it on to your children. Regardless of how rough or easy the path was I was blessed to be on this journey just as I am with my business.

May your journey into and through entrepreneurship fill your heart and mind with a sense of real accomplishment. May your dreams and hard work lead to much success, joy and happiness. May you leave a legacy that you are proud of and that makes you look back on your life and say "I had a beautiful life and lived my dreams."

Remember, success is not final and failure is not fatal.

CHAPTER 1

Getting Started

The most difficult thing is the decision to act, the rest is merely tenacity.

   - Amelia Earhart

Every great dream begins with a dreamer. Always remember, you have within you the strength, the patience, and the passion to reach for the stars to change the world.

- Harriet Tubman

Being an entrepreneur takes a very special kind of person. Some people are born with it and some people have to work extremely hard at becoming entrepreneurial. An entrepreneur is someone who will build a business using pure tenacity and vision. They will turn a mere idea into an empire. An entrepreneur may not be the smartest person and they may not be the most educated but they definitely have the most vision and the most tenacity. Being an entrepreneur means that you will get knocked down – you will get knocked down many times. You will be told that that's a silly idea or someone else is already doing it. There will likely be doubters and haters everywhere. They are entitled to their opinion but that is exactly what it is, their opinion. Find your tribe, those who believe in you and your abilities and who support you. These are the people who will keep you going.

Just know this…. There are no bad ideas- only poor execution. Find what you are passionate about and do it. The money and success will follow if you are doing what you are passionate about. Your passion will drive you, inspire you and keep you pushing forward when times get tough and when things seem hopeless. Your passion is the single most important thing that will keep you inspired in the best of times and keep you pushing ahead in the worst of times. Passion is something that comes from deep within you. It is a strong desire that can get you to do amazing things regardless of the circumstances. When you have passion for something, you love it even when you hate it.

Without action, your passion will stay dormant and nothing will come of it. The world will not end if you do not follow your passion but your chance to fuel your soul and leave your mark on this world will wither away. That would be a great disservice to you and to all that your passion will eventually touch. With this being said, only a few will leave the traditional corporate structure and venture out on their own. Not everyone is cut out to be an entrepreneur; it takes a very special type of person to become not just an entrepreneur but a successful entrepreneur. I believe entrepreneurs are to be admired and looked up to as they are the backbone of America. This country is built on entrepreneurs that turned their dreams into businesses. They create and innovate. They hire and train. They are your neighbors and friends and other members of your community.

Besides passion, anyone starting a business must be fearless. You are walking into the unknown, often with little to no resources. Many times, it is an asset to you to have limited resources in the beginning. What? Yes, you heard me. Having limited resources will force you to get smarter and more strategic and it will force you to think out of the box. This is often what makes a great business and a great business person. Have you heard the saying, "Invention is the mother of necessity"? So many great things come out of necessity and that includes running a business on a shoestring. When you are forced to do it with fewer resources you tend to get smarter and more strategic, you tend to sharpen your skills and become more innovative and see things in a new light. You learn some incredibly valuable skills and one of them is what I like to call "The Art of Unwavering Tenacity". Entrepreneurs do not give up. If one road is blocked then they take another and another and another until they get to where they need to go or they get what it is that they need. The difference between success and failure is just trying one more time and then one more after that and never giving up.

Do not let others sway you, discourage you or make you question your commitment. I can't even tell you how many times people tried to discourage me or how many times I heard that there is already someone doing what I was doing. Wow! Since when is there only one of anything?? If that were the case then we would all be driving a Ford today and none of the other auto brands would exist. Remember that you are capable and all businesses started with a single idea and someone with a passion or desire to try something or to make something better. With this being said, it is important to do your homework and know what has already been done. Do not reinvent the wheel unless the whole wheel needs redoing, which it usually does not. Use secondary research to use information that other companies have spent extensive amounts of money on. Take advantage of the road they have already paved and use your talent and tenacity to make it better.

You are much stronger than you think. The fact that you are an entrepreneur or are considering starting your own business makes you part of an incredibly special and select group of people that have that extra something that is the basis our country and economy. You are an innovator, a creator, a trailblazer, a trendsetter, a job creator, a leader and an initiator of progress. Small business owners are what this country is built on. We are the foundation. We make this country more innovative, more creative; we make it more of everything.

Regardless of your business or path, being an entrepreneur will change you. It will make you smarter and more resilient and more strategic if you let it. Don't let the challenges and adversities of building your own business change you for the worse. Use it to your advantage and know that you are stronger than most and you are amazing. You are now the master of your own destiny. How many people can say that? How many people wake up in the morning, or in my case in the middle of the night, excited and with a mind full of possibilities for the day ahead? With ideas and thoughts of building something amazing? Entrepreneurs, that's who.

Go forth and create. Change the world. Leave your mark.

CHAPTER 2

Building a Team

You know, as most entrepreneurs do, that a company is only as good as its people. The hard part is building the team that will embody your company's culture and propel you forward.

       - Kathryn Minshew

Leadership is not about a title or a designation. It's about impact, influence, and inspiration. Impact involves getting results, influence is about spreading the passion you have for your work, and you have to inspire team-mates and customers.

- Robin S. Sharma

All successful startups and businesses have one thing in common – a strong core team and a dynamic and effective leader. What would Apple be without the vision and leadership of Steve Jobs? It would be a completely different company with a different culture and who knows where mobile technology would be today if it were not for his leadership and vision. His vision and determination have changed the world in so many ways. With that being said, Steve Jobs would never have had the impact that he had without his exceptionally talented team.

Whether you have years of experience in the workforce or are a budding entrepreneur with little to no experience it is especially important to put together an incredibly strong and stable team. Entrepreneurs often ask themselves if they should build a core business team from the beginning, or try to go it alone as long as possible because they have extremely limited resources. The answer to this question can make or break a startup. The landscape in business is changing very quickly and there are so many resources that can help an entrepreneur with traditional and non-traditional staffing. These resources could help the business get going with less cash than most traditional routes.

When I started my apparel business, I was working a full-time corporate job. My apparel line was my side hustle. I spent every bit of spare time and money I had on building my company and could not afford to hire a single employee to help me. Despite being a one-man band, I marched on. I worked evenings and weekends putting my business together and designing my first collection. I found a wonderful man in downtown Los Angeles who I paid for piece work to make my patterns and samples. It was slow going but it was getting done. I look back on this time and realize how the universe brought us together. Two souls who needed each other. I know that sounds dramatic but he was new to LA and to the US. He had rented a tiny office/workroom in an old commercial building where he was hustling to get work so he too could build his business. He was working and sleeping in his office until he could make enough money to get an apartment nearby. He was a very talented tailor and designer himself. He was brilliant and I felt so lucky to find him. He told me that he was also so happy that I brought work for him to do and that he could pay rent and eat because of my work and that of a few others. It was like kismet. We needed each other and somehow in all of Los Angeles we found each other at the time when we both needed each other. We are still great friends after more than 20 years and he has built a stellar reputation and business. The universe works in very mysterious ways.

Getting a new company off the ground is a huge task and sometimes risky no matter how great an idea is, especially if there isn't anyone to help you make that dream come to life. Being able to rely on a dedicated team can help get the results you need for your business to thrive. Having the right people believe in you and your vision is vital to your business' success. Forming a sound support system of people that believe in your vision wholeheartedly will take you further than you could get trying to do it all alone.

Surrounding yourself with those who love you and believe in you is incredibly important but you will also need someone that will always tell you the truth and not just tell you what you want to hear, regardless of your feelings. This kind of honest support will make all the difference in your success but you must be prepared to be open to discussions that may be uncomfortable and make you question your direction. This is a good thing as the more you look outside of the box, the better prepared you are to build your dream.

Do yourself a favor and be realistic about what you can accomplish solo, and make a list of the things you can't do yourself. Most of us couldn't, nor should we try to fulfill all the roles of running a business unless you are planning to be a solo entrepreneur such as an independent accountant, lawyer, tennis coach, piano teacher or some other trade that would allow you to be a solo entrepreneur, or solopreneur as I like to call them.

Managing every department ourselves and trying to do so without a solid team at our back is a recipe for frustration and failure. Trying to do everything by yourself will lead to inefficiencies and hamper any potential growth, not to mention, it would be exhausting, frustrating and next to impossible. As an entrepreneur, you must focus on the big picture and not spend all of your time and resources rushing from task to task trying to do it all. Remember, you are the brains and the mind behind this business so work smarter.

Hire your core team but also surround yourself with talented experts you can trust as your business grows - experts and professionals that can handle such areas as taxes, finances, funding, etc. A great way to do this is to build an Advisory Board and fill it with mentors in the most vital areas. A big strength is recognizing when to collaborate or partner up with someone. Also know what it takes to do every job in your business, learn and understand each position. Knowing how each part of your operation works will be one of your greatest strengths as you build your company and legacy. Always know your business.

So, the real question you should be asking yourself is "How can I build the right team for my business?" and "What does the right team look like?" The right team is a strong team consisting of individual people with skills that are of value to you and your purpose. These people will truly believe in your ideas and goals, and they will want to help the business and you become successful. Their loyalty will be evident in their actions and they will be in your corner no matter what happens. That is not to say that there will not be disagreements or conflict amongst the team – there most certainly will be from time to time as we are all human and these kinds of disagreements or conflict could lead to amazing conversation and innovation if handled in a mature and professional manner. Adversity can be very good if managed properly.

A favorite saying of mine that has stayed with me for many years is "A captain does not become great by sailing in calm harbors." When you think about it, all growth comes from adversity and resistance so when things get tough just smile, buck up and remember that you are getting stronger and wiser and whatever you are going through is a great opportunity that will take you one step closer to your dream.

Let's take a look at the characteristics of a strong team.

A Strong Team Has:

Communication - An effective leader that communicates openly with employees and encourages them to do the same. A team that does not have open communication is destined to struggle and most likely fail.

Focus - Clearly defined objectives and direction from management. People work better in a more focused environment where there are visibly defined goals and clear direction from the top.

Balance - Everyone contributes and participates. A great team is a team with balance and synergy that works well together and supports the team and all of its individual members. Anyone who is not participating won't be allowed to be a slacker for long as any strong team will keep itself in check.

Support – A strong team supports and respects each other. The leader supports the team and the team supports the leader. Without this internal support and mutual respect, a team will struggle almost as if it is fighting against itself. If this inner fighting is not handled immediately then you are bound to have major struggles and strife and this is bad for you and your business. You will have enough struggles from outside so keep the inside strong and harmonious.

Positive Environment - Each team member has a positive attitude & the drive to succeed. You must create an environment where employees are happy and engaged. Look at Google and many tech startups. They know that their employees put in a ridiculous number of hours and brainpower so they have created an environment that doesn't feel so much like work. It is flexible and fun and creative and all of this nurtures their team. Employees at these companies are actually much more engaged and productive than at many traditional companies. Find what works and keep your employees engaged and they will give you 150%.

Diversity - Team members are diverse and have a wide variety of experiences and viewpoints that they can bring to the table. They can use their experience use to help team members to see another part of the business that they may not understand or may not even know exists. A team is more innovative and strategic when they understand the big picture of the business.

Synergy - Employees have varied but complementary skill sets and personalities. This is a difficult one because complementary personalities can be extremely difficult to determine upfront sometimes. Your team must work well together and have a similar work ethic for synergy to exist within the team.

Organization – The team is clearly organized and is lean. Bring on team members that add value to the team. Everyone should be able to contribute something unique and specialized. These team members will help lead the innovation and growth of your company so choose wisely. A deadweight team member will throw off the balance and synergy that a team needs to kick butt.

Peace and Harmony – Employees should all get along with one another. They do not have to be the best of friends but they do have to respect each other. Every member of your team should be confident and comfortable enough within the team to speak up even if it means going against the group. If they do, the group must be open- minded enough to listen and consider. Harmony in your team will keep it running like a well-oiled machine.

Building the Right Team

Building a solid team of core employees has never been more important to business owners and managers than it is today. With everyone having an online presence on social media it's becoming harder to get an accurate read on someone's personality right away. Their social media may show a completely different view of the person or may even make you question whether they would be a good fit before you even interview them. In my personal experience, it is better to meet them in person to see the real person behind the screen.

When say meet them, I do not mean all of them.

I would not waste one second on anyone who has posts on social media that shows something alarming such as intolerance, bullying, hatred or even worse. I have met people that had posted questionable stuff on their social media, nothing dangerous or intolerant, just questionable for a business and they have turned out to be amazing people and employees who had been pulled in by peer pressure and had posted a few things that they should probably not have posted.

Don't ignore a rough diamond. Sometimes all someone needs is for someone to believe in them and help them to get their polish on so they can sparkle.

A strong team is a harmonious team. It is no longer enough to hire people with the right qualifications, experience, and education.

Today, the way to decide whether or not to hire a particular person is by asking yourself a few questions about potential candidates. Does this new person have the potential to share your vision and enthusiasm for the success of your team? How will that additional person impact and contribute to the overall goal of your company? Will this new employee be a good personality fit within your current staff? Is it easy to communicate with the candidate, and do they fully understand what you want to accomplish for your business? Are they eager to learn and grow? Will they speak up and participate?

Hiring the right people can feel like an overwhelming and daunting task. You can choose to either dread the prospect or embrace it. Look at it as an opportunity to build your dream team filled with employees that have the skills and talent you need to make your business prosper. These people will become a second family to you. You will often spend more time with them than you spend with your friends and family.

The right employees that make up a strong team will be made up of motivated individuals that have the expertise, talents, and skills that you need to ultimately benefit the success of your business. Enthusiastic employees with positive attitudes will have a vested interest in the successfulness of your company and they will do their absolute best to be part of that success.

Choosing the Right Players

The phrase, "team player" is thrown around a lot when discussing how to build a strong core team. It is often used to describe a person that is concerned more about the greater good of an organization above their own self-serving aspirations. No one can make it to the top alone, and instead of stepping on people and using them to get what you want, value your team players and their contributions to your business' success.

Team players are essential for any business to thrive. It is important that the working environment cultivated by management support a team-building culture among their staff. Employees working effectively as part of a team is incredibly vital for product and service output quality. It can also improve company morale and even impact employee retention.

Team players believe in your cause and your ideas and are loyal to you and their colleagues. They take pride in their work and share information with each other. Surrounding yourself with skilled team players is a smart investment and a great business decision.

A strong team is the force that creates success and behind every profitable business is a core group of team players. It has been said that "although it's lonely at the top, no one gets their alone". Team players will not only help you get to the top, but they will also help you stay at the top. It is incredibly important to acknowledge their contributions and show appreciation for their efforts. It is also important to show your loyalty to your staff and make them feel secure in their job and the health of your business.

Avoiding Poisonous Personalities

We all make mistakes, which is why pencils have erasers and computers have backspaces and delete buttons. While some mistakes are bigger than others, hiring the wrong person can cost you in more ways than one. Hiring the wrong person means we were either misled by that person or we misjudged them and now have a team member who is a poor fit. Sometimes we take it personally as if it's a poor reflection of ourselves but it isn't. We just made a mistake – a very costly one. Be quick to admit your mistakes, correct them and move forward. Mistakes are the best way to learn lessons that last a lifetime.

I remember one of the worst hires I have ever made. He came to me through a referral from the local college and I hired him without as much due diligence as I should have done because he came to me through a referral. Big mistake! This guy, we will call him Employee X, would show up late and then spend most of his day hiding out texting with his fiancée. He would even go into the bathroom for upwards of 20 minutes with his phone to text. This caused me to institute a strict cell phone policy meaning everyone had to suffer because of his behavior.

Employee X was late several more times so I wrote him up and warned him. Even after the warning he continued to be late, almost as if daring me to do something. It was not long before his final warning came, as I knew it would, and I had to fire him. He had caused so much disruption in my business and with other employees that I was not sad to see him go, especially when he uttered these words after I fired him for being over an hour late, "What's the big deal? Don't make an issue of this." After I refused to continue the discussion with him, I received the text stating, "Please do not make problems." Wow!

Employee X took a long time to go away. Even after I told him in no uncertain terms that I would not reconsider he would not go away. He even went so far as to contact my previous office manager and ask her to write him a letter on my company letterhead. She forwarded his communication to me immediately and he finally went away when he knew he was out of options with me. Not only did this employee take up a lot of my time and aggravate me, he disrupted my team and caused discord where there had never been any. After Employee X was let go, the harmony returned to my team and everyone was back to normal. I was especially lucky as this is not always the case. The team may not always go back to the better place when things like this happen. I was very fortunate to not lose any employees during this time. When you think about costs think about this, aggravation is one of the largest expenses in any business.

When hiring new employees, never settle for someone simply to fill a spot. Sometimes we get lucky, but most of the time that hasty decision will create an even bigger problem. Many problems stem from hiring the wrong person.

Two of the main problems that stem from hiring the wrong person that could hurt your team are:

1. They may only do the bare minimum that is necessary to get by which will most likely cause a great deal of discord, and

2. They may not want to be a part of a team, constantly behaving as a solo member instead of a team member, causing friction among your team where there initially was none.

Hiring an employee who is either one of these will be toxic to your team and will end up "poisoning the well" - killing morale with super speed and precision which in turn could derail your business. Your team represents you and your business. It is one of the greatest assets you can have when building and running a business.

Choosing someone for a permanent position who you aren't entirely thrilled about will only be counterproductive and more times than not, that choice will immediately backfire. If you are unable to find a permanent employee with the right qualifications and the right attitude, consider hiring a freelancer, intern or a consultant in the interim. This will be beneficial for everyone since you will get to test-drive the candidate and their skills. The try before you buy route is often a good idea because you will get to see that employee in action without making the huge commitment of assigning them to a permanent place among your staff until you have a solid idea of who they are. Hopefully, they will mesh well with the other members of your team and you will see if their talent and skills live up to the expectation. This will also allow you to get a better handle on their personality and an idea of the kind of employee they will be, all with minimal commitment.

While in the trial period with a freelancer, intern or consultant, ask some of your trusted employees for their feedback on that person's work and how they feel about working with them on projects. Encourage them to be completely candid about how they feel and keep their answers in mind when considering that temporary employee for a permanent position. Ask them if the new team member is pulling their weight and if that new employee is a strong team member or not. If it doesn't work out for some reason, you only need to terminate the contract and cut your losses without investing too much time, energy, and money into the wrong person. On the other hand, if it does work out, and they prove to be a valuable part of the team, consider hiring them.

Once you feel confident that the potential employee could be an asset and your team and you are comfortable with their personality, offer them a permanent position on your staff and be glad that you took a calculated chance on the right person. I have had several instances where I hired interns into permanent roles within the company. Two of them stand out more than the others. They were excellent team players and had fantastic work ethic. They were a great fit to the team and became extremely valuable long-term employees. I probably would have not found either of them had I not first brought them in as interns. To this day I still am in contact with them and am so thrilled with every milestone that they reach in their careers and personal lives. I even recently visited one of them in Turkey.

On the other hand, if you get a negative vibe from a potential employee, or you are on the fence about hiring them for any reason, err on the side of caution and don't hire them.

Your team should consist of valuable people that support you and believe in you – not people who will drag you down and hold you back or cause you undue stress. Team members are not just people who work for you; they are your friends and family – anyone who supports you. It is very difficult to do but try to avoid those who make you feel guilty about not spending more time with them when you're trying to get your business off the ground. It may sound harsh, but when you are just starting, your business will have to be your main focus. The right people will understand and support you while pursuing your dream and it will be such a treat to be encouraged by the ones you know love you and cheer you on day in and day out during the early days of your company. Those who truly care about you will want you to be successful.

Diversity and team building

Diversity among your team is exceptionally helpful to a successful business. People bring all of who they are to a team and having a group of people with different backgrounds will only enhance your team's capabilities. Research suggests that companies with both male and female executives and/or board members financially outperform companies with all-male executives or board members. It also shows that companies with diverse cultures and backgrounds tend to be more successful and creative. A diverse and multicultural team can offer different perspectives that could be exceptionally valuable in the creative and problem-solving process.

Culture transcends all parts of life including the way we work. When you have employees from different countries, races, religions, backgrounds, and cultures, a leader needs to find ways to balance those differences so that the team works well together. As long as team members can work as a cohesive unit and respect one another, a smart leader can harness the power of diverse thought and use it to accomplish goals quicker than a group of the same type of people. At the end of the day, your team players will be collaborating and working together—all with a common objective, actively striving to achieve the ultimate goal of success. Building a diverse team is a good business decision and can bring much more to your business than a homogenous team ever could. It can also greatly broaden your horizons and viewpoints.

The bottom line for teams

By working in teams, employees can contribute to cost savings for the company - improved skill sets, lower employee turnover rates, and increased productivity are just a few of those benefits of working with a strong team. Hire people who will genuinely care about the success of your company. Choose people that will bring out the best in each other and who will put forth the effort to meet and even exceed your expectations. In the age of limitless information and short attention spans, we can forget the most basic principles of what takes individuals and transforms them into a successful team. We need to be able to sift through all the various layers of personality traits and find a common thread among a group of individual people, a common purpose, and then go for it. Be sure, before you hire them, that these are people that will support your vision and respect your dream. Don't forget to surround yourself with those who love you and will always tell you the truth.

Now that we know about building a team, let's take a look at leadership. After all, what is a team without a great leader?

CHAPTER 3

THE EFFECTIVE LEADER

The first step to solving any problem is to accept one's own accountability for creating it

- Stan Slap

One of the most significant barriers to progress is the lack of effective leadership

- Ken Jennings

Before you start putting your dream team together you should first take an honest assessment of yourself. You should identify your strengths and weaknesses and list the skills that you lack so you can get a clear grasp of exactly what skills you will be looking for in potential employees. You should also truly evaluate how many employees you need, part-time, full-time and virtual.

Once you are honest about who and what you need to turn your idea into a business and to make your dream a reality, focus on laying the groundwork to develop a strong team of smart, talented, loyal and driven people. Remember that your ego can be your downfall if not kept in check. Be honest with yourself, even if you do not like the answers but also do not downplay your value and skills.

An effective leader has the respect of their employees – respect that has been earned over time and is rooted in trust and a common belief in the business. Having your team trust you and your judgment is not an easy thing to accomplish and is not to be taken for granted. For instance, if you are running a small business or a startup, you need to keep in mind that the people you hire will be relying on you for their livelihood and for fulfilling and challenging work. Conversely, you will be relying on them to do the things you need to be done for your business to be successful.

This does not just mean completing tasks; it also means sharing their ideas and experiences. Remember that employees are people with very real feelings and needs, not just tools. People respond better to leaders that support them and acknowledge their needs as well. The employer/employee relationship is one of mutual respect, and in the long run, that respect and support will be one of the best investments you can make in your business. Your success is their success and vice versa.

When asked what they feel is the most important attribute that their manager could possess, employees resoundingly respond with something so simple, it's often overlooked – an open line of communication. Of all the characteristics managers and leaders are known for, employees most often comment and complain about the lack of communication from their supervisors and upper management. Employees that feel like they are in the loop are far more likely to stay engaged in their job and truly care about the quality of their work. Communicating your ambitions to your team and expressing your expectations clearly is one of the most underrated actions a leader can use to perfect a successful team. Fortunately, the request for increased communication is something that owners and managers can easily fix - usually with no increase in costs. The return on this investment is invaluable.

An Active Leader with a Positive Attitude

An involved leader with an open door and a positive attitude is paramount for your business to thrive and evolve properly. If your employees feel as though you are just as interested as they are in their work, they will be more likely to be passionate about their projects and the positivity will produce much greater results than those of an employee that feels isolated. Everyone likes to be recognized and respected. Everyone wants to be heard. This is not a difficult thing for a leader to do and it costs absolutely nothing. It will bring about vast returns to your company via the engagement, productivity, and retention of your employees.

Employees feel more attuned to each other and their managers when the manager plays an active role in directing the team by setting clear expectations and timeframes for each project or assignment. Being vague with your expectations or being seemingly unavailable to your employees will create problems within your group and essentially ruin morale and kill motivation. Doing the bare minimum for your employees will only get you bare minimum results from your team, because after all, why should they care if you don't. It all goes back to the old adage, "you reap what you sow". Plant the seeds and water them and tend to them with great care and they will grow into fruitful strong trees.

As a leader with a strong team, you must still stay involved with the day to day operations as much as possible. Do so without micromanaging your employees or getting in the way of their productivity. Be a positive influence for your employees to aspire to and support them by guiding them when they need it. On the flip side, if they are "in the zone", try to give them space to do their thing and offer feedback when they ask for it.

Show your employees that you appreciate their efforts and acknowledge their commitment to the success of the company. Offering praise when your employees accomplish important milestones is a simple way of maintaining a positive atmosphere and perpetuating high morale throughout the company. Acknowledgment of their contributions to the success of your business is a step in the right direction and adds to the give-and-take relationship of employer and employee. This type of involvement is vital to earning the trust and loyalty of your employees and isn't easily substituted by pay alone.

Being an involved leader while demonstrating a positive attitude will generate the type of energy needed to lead your company to the success you are aiming for. If given a choice, people will always prefer to work with an optimistic and open leader rather than a sarcastic or pessimistic or egotistical leader- even if the pay is less. Optimism is contagious in the best possible way and has a proven track record of boosting employee productivity. Having happy employees is not a myth and you have a far better chance of building a strong team if you have a positive attitude and provide open communication and support for your team.

A strong team is imperative but there is so much more to building a successful business. Regardless of what you have been told, there is no one set path, map or rule-book that will definitively lead you and your business to success. There are formulas that work to help you be successful but every business is different and has many different nuances, the most unpredictable and most powerful one being the human factor. Be engaged and involved in your business at all levels. Know every job and facet of your business - at least a little.

Never stop asking yourself, "Would I hire me?" "Would I buy this product or service?" If you are honest with yourself the answer may be no for a while. Figure out what will make that answer a yes and get to it.

CHAPTER 4

Run Your Business As If You Are Broke

Rule No.1: Never lose money. Rule No.2: Never forget rule No.1.

    - Warren Buffett

Always deliver more than expected.

-         Larry Page, co-founder of Google

So, you want to start a new business, but you don't have the money to do it – or so you think you don't have the money to do it. Most of us cannot, nor should we just up and quit our job today armed with only an idea for a new business. While that does sound appealing, most of us don't have the financial freedom to do so and we depend on the income from our jobs to support ourselves and our families. That doesn't mean you shouldn't try to start a business, but it does mean you should be realistic about what you need to do in order to get started without any startup money of your own. I started my business while working a corporate job in healthcare. It was not easy but it was a lot easier than trying to do it without a steady paycheck to cover my necessities. Start smart to give yourself a better chance of success.

 There are two main reasons people don't start a business: one is the fear of failing, and the other reason is money, or rather the lack thereof. It may be hard to believe but there are lots of options available, and you should consider each one carefully before you enter the role of entrepreneur and take that step to launch a business. Every successful business started from an idea and then a plan – and you can do it too.

You can start a business with only a small amount of money, and sometimes, no money at all. The amount of startup money you will need all depends on the type of business you are starting. Starting a service or consulting business will require the least amount of monetary investment. On the other hand, if you are starting a clothing line, opening a store or doing anything else that requires manufacturing or inventory then you will absolutely need capital to get started.

With any business, you will require a minimal investment to put together your branding and marketing materials. With the popularity of sites like Freelancer and Fiverr and Upwork you can get logos and graphics done as well as websites built for a small investment. Some printers are small business-friendly like Smart Levels Media. They have incredibly diverse product offerings and their printing costs rival almost anyone who I have used or researched over the years. Business cards, brochures, fliers and practically anything else you need to get started are so reasonably priced. I know there are a few online that are cheaper but their products look cheap to me. Some of them even put their logo on the back of your business card!! What? Every product I have ever ordered from Smart Levels Media has looked like a million bucks and absolutely no one believes how little I paid. Full disclosure, I have been a paying customer of Smart Levels and Freelancer for years. I am not receiving any compensation or favor for mentioning them in this book. I am mentioning them merely because they are so awesome and they have helped my business to grow with all of the great printed materials and graphics work that I have ordered (and paid for) throughout the years.

Back to the issue of money, money is one of the few infinite commodities in the world and it can be unlimited for you too if you build your business properly. With the right strategy and mindset, your earning potential is unlimited. To build a business and bring in the money you must invest your time and energy in addition to your money, and any other resources you have at your disposal. The struggle will be extremely real but you will have a purpose, and the reward is financial freedom - being your own boss, running your business how you want to run it, and quitting your day job once your business is profitable enough to support your lifestyle. Do not quit your day job before your business is able to sustain itself and able to support you and your living necessities. I know it is tempting but the income and benefits that you get from your day job will be so important to you while you are building your business. The comfort of knowing that you have a paycheck coming every couple of weeks and that you have good health and dental insurance will make you that much more focused on building and growing your business.

Plan your strategy meticulously and do your research on your business model and make a list of all things you will need to put your plan into motion. That should include finding out if you need any type of licenses, permits or insurance policies in order to operate your business. Being realistic and practicing patience will net you success – but you have to be smart about your startup to get things off the ground. You should keep working at your current job to support yourself while spending time working on your business after-hours and weekends. You should also get comfortable with the idea of living like you are broke in order to put whatever cash you do have to good use and make your money work for you. Remember those days when you were broke? So broke you had to scrounge for change or juggle bills to keep going? This is how it often is when you start a business. You will run your business being broke for a while, but you have to start somewhere. Even when your new business starts being profitable you should still run your business as if you are still broke by reinvesting your profits to grow your business.

Avoid unnecessary spending by asking yourself what you absolutely need to operate your new business. Do you really need that fancy office space? NO. Do you need to hire a bunch of employees to start? NO. Do you need the fanciest computer or printer? Probably not, but maybe - every purchase should be thought out with a shoestring budget in mind and a true idea of what you really need to do your job and build your business. Consider the return on investment when spending your hard-earned money since what you will spend will depend on the nature of your business and what you need to have to run it properly. In order to build a business and bring in enough money to keep it going, you must invest time, money and resources. Start-up costs are categorized as part of cost centers – which means they cost money, but they don't make money. You want to try to make every department a profit center instead of a cost center and keep costs in check. But if you are savvy you will not have to invest much money on things that will not bring in money. There are so many resources today that it is not necessary to spend a huge amount of money getting a business started. You can, and should, use the multitude of resources available to you which will allow you to build your business on a shoestring.

A profit center makes you money. It has positive cash flow.

Don't spend money frivolously; don't spend money unless you need to. Money is a resource and should be treated as such. Ask yourself, Will this purchase make me money? Every dollar you spend should net you at least $2 in return and it is not only about the resources but also very much about your resourcefulness.

For some types of businesses equipment and tools are important, and you need them to be successful - so invest in them but invest wisely. For example, if you are setting up a new house cleaning service, you may need an industrial- strength vacuum, but rather than forking out hundreds of dollars to buy one before you have any revenue or clients, rent one only when you need it instead and do that until you've made enough money and have enough regular customers to buy an industrial vacuum cleaner. You could also cut costs simply by buying the store brand or generic cleaning supplies instead of the name brand. Look for sales and coupons - it is all free money that you can use to grow your business. A dollar saved can turn into ten dollars when invested back into the business.

Statistically, 9 out of 10 new businesses fail within the first year because they lack the capital to get through the initial year. So, by having little or no overhead costs, you can be the exception to that rule. If you believe in your idea or product you can make it happen. Have clearly defined goals and a strong business model before trying to fund your new business – this will set you on the path to getting what you want. Take a gamble on yourself and your idea, you can and will succeed where others have failed – even on a shoestring budget.

There are plenty of businesses that you can start that utilize your best assets – your mind, your talent, and your skills. Get creative, and create a business that you want to build. Grow at your own pace, and don't let the lack of upfront capital hold you back. Starting small and taking the temperature of the industry you are interested in joining by dipping a proverbial toe in, is a good idea when starting.

Many well-known companies started with meager beginnings, and setting up shop at your home can be quite lucrative. In fact, Apple, Amazon, and Google all started in garages and they are three of the most recognizable brands in the world now. Spanx was started in a home and meetings were held at her kitchen table. Have you ever heard of Subway? Of course you have! It was founded by two guys and only $1,000 in seed money. Where there is passion and tenacity there is the possibility for anything.

Some entrepreneurs like cosmetologists, hairdressers, and estheticians often work out of their homes or are mobile. Personal chefs and diet delivery services are more popular than ever before – so if you're a good cook, you can start small and the only money needed upfront will be on food and container costs. These people aren't afraid to hustle, they operate after hours and on weekends, growing their clientele and building their brand. This enables them to run their business on the side until they are making enough money to quit their jobs and focus on growing their business and being their own boss full time.

Freelancing and consulting work has exploded the last few years and has created the "Gig Lifestyle". The gig lifestyle is gaining popularity because of its flexibility and low or no overhead cost to the freelancer. The gig lifestyle is trending as another way for people to make money on the side by using the skills and talents they already have. There is NO overhead for office space or employees to pay - and you can do it whenever you want, and how often you want. The gig lifestyle is all about freelancing and consulting services and it is fast becoming an easy way for people to enter the realm of being self-employed while not investing any money on cost centers. While renting traditional office space was a necessity less than a decade ago, today, due to the rise of virtual office services and co-working spaces, working from home or your favorite coffee shop or café with free Wi-Fi is the new norm, and is widely accepted by professionals throughout many industries.

There are lots of reputable sites to match up clients to the right freelancer and many of the sites vet both the freelancer and the clients to provide security for each party and to also ensure that the client and freelancer both get what they want. Most of these sites take a percentage of your earnings, but it's worth it because you know that you'll be paid for your work, and it has the added bonus of not costing you a penny upfront. They provide the platform, do all of the marketing and bring the customer and freelancer together. You would have to pay a considerable amount more to do all of this and even then you most likely would not be able to do it to the level that they already are. Do not try to do everything the hard way. Be resourceful. It will save you a lot of time, money, resources and most importantly aggravation.

Make a website using a free platform like WordPress or GoDaddy GoCentral, use a free shopping cart like WooCommerce and accept payments using stripe or square or PayPal instead of paying monthly fees to get a merchant account. Once you are set up you can start campaigning for new clients and customers. Put yourself out there and see if you get any bites, then start building your reputation thru your customers and clients, asking for referrals and attending small business networking events in your community. You can also ask friends and family to vouch for you in the form of testimonials. Video testimonials are always better as they are more authentic while many written ones may appear fabricated or made up. Another way to get the attention and business you seek is to just pick up the phone and call. Yes, you can call Costco buyers or call any large company but do your homework before you do. The internet has almost anything that you may need to do your due diligence. It will only annoy the buyer if you are pitching them on items that they do not carry or are pitching them when you do not have your business affairs in order. Some large companies require that you have a minimum amount of revenue or a certain time in business before they will meet with you. Be prepared and start dialing. When you start reaching out to these large companies, it may take a while to get to the person that you need to talk to or you may not reach them at all. What do you have to lose by picking up the phone? If nothing else, you have gained experience and are learning how to do it better next time. Many large companies respect your initiative when you reach out to them directly. You have to remember that they have a job to do as well and might be looking for what you have to offer. Put yourself out there and you may just surprise yourself

Freelancing is easier than ever before now that people can connect online from anywhere around the world, offering remote services to anyone they see fit. Micro gigs are more profitable than people think and it also enables freelancers to make their own hours, set their own prices, and choose what they want to work on. Using your talents and expertise to make money in your spare time is rewarding in several ways. It will help you build a solid clientele, and it can fund your life – all without costing any money upfront.

Web consulting freelance work is becoming more and more popular and there are multiple sites online to help web consultants and other freelancers find work like web design, graphic design, and copywriting just to name a few. Offering consulting services, like legal advice, or tax advice can also be done now without the expense of a brick and mortar office. Using web conferencing for legal advice, tax prep services, and even life-coaching is now socially acceptable and can be a serious moneymaker if you put the effort and time into it. Since you can do this kind of work whenever you want, you can go at your own pace until your business is profitable enough to cover the overhead required to run the business and cover your expenses. This will allow you to support yourself (and your family) fully.

Sites like TheSelfEmployed.com is a web portal for the self-employed. The site is a one-stop-shop for everything you need to know to have a successful entrepreneurial journey. On it, you will find relevant articles, how-to videos, podcasts, forums, and special offers that are all designed specifically for the self-employed. Another great site is TaskRabbit.com, it matches up customers with self-employed people to get smaller jobs done. Using these sites to build your business could be especially helpful as they could facilitate getting your small business started. These sites, and others like them, are often an untapped resource for new businesses without capital.

On the other hand, if your business will be providing a product of some kind, you'll need to take a different route because seed money is necessary to produce or purchase your product or products. Fear not! There are several ways to go about getting that money to start a business that requires an initial investment of capital.

The most common option for securing capital is a bank or getting a small business loan. Going to banks that are backed by the Small Business Administration (SBA) is usually the first stop once you have your business model planned out and a design or a prototype of the product you want to bring to market in hand. A strong business plan is key here. Getting a bank or SBA loan has gotten increasingly more difficult since banks have tightened up lending after the banking and mortgage crisis. Another tip is to start out applying for your small business loan at smaller community banks and credit unions first, as they tend to approve more small business loans over the bigger banks that prefer bigger already established profitable customers. People tend to think that applying for a business loan is difficult and frustrating, but it's easier than most think. If you need that seed money to get your business going it will be worth the time and effort it takes to put together a sound business plan, dress professionally, fill out those forms and set up a meeting with the loan officer at the local bank or credit union.

Sites like Kickstarter.com and GoFundMe.com offer crowdsourcing to promising inventors, filmmakers, artists, and other creative aspiring entrepreneurs. Anyone with the means, which often starts at a very small amount, can invest in your company in the early stages in exchange for the item being created or a small stake in the company itself. While crowdfunding is a viable option – remember that you must be prepared to produce and ship the goods you are promoting or even give investors a piece of your company in exchange for their investment in financing your dream. The good news is that you decide what your offering will be and you still maintain control of your company if you plan the offering properly. You'll maintain control over your entire operation as the online investors are most often of the silent variety.

Starting a business of any kind is always a risk versus reward situation. Unfortunately, people inherently tend to associate risk with fear and ignore the reward aspect to avoid failing at all. Focus on risk versus reward rather than letting the fear of failure determine your future. It's pretty simple, if you fail to plan, you'll fail. But if you plan to succeed – then you'll succeed. Your money should make you money and should buy you the ultimate commodity – time. The big secret that you most likely never learned as a child or even as an adult is that you should spend your money-making time, not spend your time making money. Confusing, huh? Lots of us have been taught that if you work harder and longer than everyone else that you will move ahead and make more money. Well, that is not exactly true. It does happen but why would you work selling your time when you can work selling your mind? When you can help others solve their problems? When you can be the master of your own destiny?

A business is always moving. It is never stable. It is either growing or it is dying.

CHAPTER 5

Do What You Do Best

Definiteness of purpose is the starting point of all achievement.
- W. Clement Stone

What I wanted was to be allowed to do the thing in the world that I did best—which I believed then and believe now is the greatest privilege there is. When I did that, success found me

- Debbie Fields

If it were somehow possible to get access to an archive of the real-life experience of the men and women who have shaped the business world through their ideas and actions, then there is a high probability that what you will find will broaden your mind and make you rethink your approach to business. A common denominator amongst highly successful people in business is the fact that they channel their efforts into things they know how to do best. They direct their activities, study, money, and network into areas where they are confident of leveraging their wealth of experience. Then, they back it up with hard work and determination.It could be an arduous task trying to attain lasting success and fulfillment doing something you don't really love. It may be possible to achieve career success doing what you don't know how to do very well when working for someone else. But as an entrepreneur, choosing an area where you cannot apply your strengths will most likely leave you with many problems which could be a recipe for disaster.

In the cases of the successful people that were mentioned in the opening paragraph, one thing is common and that's functional expertise. They have a specific skill or range of skills that they are extremely good at. This expertise could be in the customer relationship, product development, finance, operations, marketing, strategy, design, etc. It could be in any area of business. There is always one thing these exceptionally successful people are highly skilled at. Some may be good at assembling the best minds or team to bring a dream to fruition, while some may be experts at getting money out of the hands of the most frugal investor. There is no limit to these skills. And the most successful entrepreneurs have one or more of these skills that have been honed to perfection. A skill that they are passionate about and drives them day in and day out to push forward towards success.

For example, Mark Zuckerberg was first a programmer and so was Larry Page, Bill Gates, and Steve Jobs. They were extremely good at coding and that's what made them stand out in the first place. Eventually, they had to develop other skills that made them incredibly successful at building and running multi-billion-dollar businesses. But before they made it big, there was something that they excelled at, and this is what paved the way for the opportunity to create their billion-dollar organizations, even as they had to start developing other important skills along the way. Passion for what you do well gives you a major advantage and takes you closer to innovation, growth, and success.

Before Elon Musk started Tesla and Space X, he was a co-founder of PayPal, an electronic payment solutions site. A sharp look at his business trajectory shows that he is good at developing tech-based businesses. Oprah Winfrey has always loved television and she worked at a TV station before owning her own TV show and going into syndication. She knows the TV business well and her experience as an employee at a TV station was instrumental to the success of her highly popular show, Oprah. Also, she listened to smart people who had skills that she lacked. Movie critic Roger Ebert told her that she should go into syndication with her show. She did and it led her to become the Oprah that we all know and love today.

Steve Jobs loved marketing and design and that's how the iPhone was able to change the world of mobile devices and what they were capable of doing. During Job's lifetime, the iPhone was considered by tech pundits as the best designed mobile phone ever. His eye for design and his vision changed the world of mobile communication forever and forced other companies to step up their development and innovation.

The CEO of Whole Foods, John Mackey has always had an eye for good food and it led him to cofound the natural foods grocery giant. Food is what he knows and food is where he maintains and continues to build his empire. Whole Foods was acquired by Amazon for approximately $14 billion. This is what following your passion and doing what you do best can bring forth. Granted, this is not the norm but it is definitely not impossible. Don't give up. Keep pushing ahead.

There are countless other stories of people who do what they do best and are super successful at it. Some you will hear about but most of them you will never hear a word about or know their name. These entrepreneurs are your neighbors, your sister's friend, the lady next to you on the plane, the man behind you at the grocery store. The truth is that everyone starts their journey with an idea or a dream and everyone's journey is unique. While the opportunity is there, only a small percentage of entrepreneurs end up becoming so successful that they become a household name or the face of an entire industry. While there are many factors involved in becoming this successful, one of the main factors is that somewhere along the line, these people are able to figure out their strengths. They figure out exactly the one or two things that they know how to do best and they do them with such passion and tenacity – and they never give up. This changes everything for them and those who work with them and for them. These people are the ones who are unstoppable.

While it is may be easy to assume that once you get functional expertise, everything will fall into place and you will become highly successful, that is not extremely common. Finding what you know how to do best is more of the beginning than the end of it. Figuring out what you know how to do best is just one step, but it is an exceptionally large step that becomes the foundation of everything else. The natural progression will be to find that area where you can put this skill to work—the area of business that will make good and productive use of this skill.

This is where things get a little bit more difficult. A little more difficult because figuring out what you know how to do best could be challenging in itself, especially if you are quite good at several things. If you find yourself in this dilemma, it is quite helpful to look at all the business endeavors that you have been in previously and do a strength and weakness analysis. Take a look at scenarios where you have excelled and think about the actions you took. The same goes for the unsuccessful ones too. If you have no business experience, then this is the time to take action. An eaglet will not know it can fly if it never tries.

If you already know what your strength is and have figured out your functional expertise, then go ahead to do an analysis of businesses that would allow you to apply this skill or interest. The search process itself may open your eyes to a lot of ideas and opportunities that you never knew existed. If you have already figured out that functional expertise and have found an area where it can be further groomed or can catapult you to a bigger platform, then it's time to give your all and go into business.

It's a good feeling to wake up on your terms and dictate the terms of business as one deems fit. But before you get to that stage where you have all that freedom, something has to give—and that's your tenacity and hard work. Failure is also part of the process. If it was easy, everyone would be Arianna Huffington, JK Rowling, Steve Jobs or Michael Dell. Now, no one is saying sleepless nights are a prerequisite for success, but quick and easy success will most likely not happen. You have to develop your willpower and resilience. This will be an extremely interesting journey but it will change your life because as an entrepreneur you are in control—and you are wielding a lot of control. Use it wisely and do not let it give you a false sense of security or ego. Being careless and reckless with your control could turn out to be your downfall if you are not careful.

There are so many great things about being an entrepreneur. There are also so many challenging things. No one is going to make you read a book or industry news, attend an industry event, or engage customers or do the many tedious tasks that come with owning and running a business. This is what makes it challenging. You call the shots and have the freedom but everything is also on you; you carry the weight of the entire business. The risk and the benefit are all yours. Be wise and learn from every possible source and experience. This will make you much wiser and a much better entrepreneur.

This brings us back to the point of persistence, hard work and the will to surmount challenges and failures that you will most certainly encounter. Many people will not see you do all of this and it's OK. People only see the tip of the iceberg; they never see the huge mass that lies beneath. Your long hours, failures, successes, disappointments, persistence, consistency, long nights, late nights, overwhelming moments, and moments where you have to second-guess your abilities and your actions are things that are mostly all in the background and things that most will never see or know about. What they see is the finished product or the fully stocked store. They don't know what they don't know. I also produce fashion shows in

Southern California for charity and if everyone saw all of the sweat it takes to make these shows happen and the chaos that goes on backstage up until the show starts, they would never stay and see the beautiful show. They come for the entertainment and to see a beautifully polished show. They do not want to see the nitty-gritty of it. People know you by your finished product so make sure that you put in the effort to make sure they get what they are paying for, the polished finished product.

To be a successful entrepreneur, you may need to make some changes and accept certain facts. You must believe in yourself while giving yourself room for improvement. You will hit brick walls occasionally. But you must be persistent, dedicated, and disciplined. Being broke also comes with the territory. But still, you will need to take action in spite of your fears. Consistency of these actions will come in handy on days when you don't feel like fighting the fight. Unknowns will come and you will encounter failure along the way but you will need to keep going no matter what. Sometimes, you may feel unqualified for these goals, but it is these goals that force you to become a bigger and smarter person than you ever imagined yourself to be.

CHAPTER 6

Know Your Customer and Your Market

We've had three big ideas at Amazon that we've stuck with for 18 years, and they're the reason we're successful:

Put the customer first. Invent.

And be patient.

> - Jeff Bezos

There is only one boss - The customer. And he can fire everybody in the company from the chairman on down, simply by spending his money somewhere else.

- Sam Walton

This is probably the most used cliché in the history of business clichés: "The customer is always right". It is the most used because the customer is your business. They are what allow you to keep producing goods or services. Without them, there is no business. The biggest threat of all is that they have many options and they will exercise those options if you do not take care of them and make them feel valued and important to you. There will always be nasty customers who may not be justified in their complaint, but knowing how to solve your customers' issues no matter how irrational their requests are can go a long way in helping you reach your business goals and build a strong customer base. Handling a customer in the right way, whether they are right or wrong, justified or not, could bring you lifelong loyalty or an awfully angry ex-customer who will tell any and everyone who will listen how horrible your company and/or product is.

In my industry, wholesale and retail, it is common that customers generally want the best product for the best price. They want the quality of a Bentley for the price of a Ford. They want the best value for their money. There is also a segment of customers who don't typically think this way. These customers are those that purchase high- end luxury goods as a rule. For them, the more expensive a product is and the more exclusive, the more they want it as it portrays a certain status and position in society. It makes them feel a certain way to know that they can afford goods that most people cannot. This is why manufacturers of luxury goods ensure that they only create a limited number of products because an expensive product, an exclusive product, a product that is considered a luxury item should be limited and create a demand. Since scarcity drives demand, they are often able to grow their business and build a following. People want what others cannot have. This has been a very successful business model for many designer product manufacturers such as Prada, Louis Vuitton, Chanel, along with many others. These goods are rarely, if ever, discounted. The brand must maintain their exclusivity and status or risk losing their customer.

One thing is crystal clear regardless of what your product or price points are: there is a vital need to know your customers and understand their needs better than even they do. You need to know what they want, what they really really want. By this I mean, yes, they may want shoes but understanding exactly what kind of shoes and what they will use them for and how often they will wear them and every single detail about what the customer wants and needs – even understanding things that your customer doesn't know about themselves is understanding what they really want. Anticipate their needs. You can only do this is if you truly understand your customer.

Understanding the demographics of your customers and designing your marketing and products for that demographic is vital to the success of your business. Is your product most suitable for millennials? Or Generation X? or Men? Or Kids? How much do you think people in this group are willing to pay? Do you think people in slightly higher demographics can easily relate to it? Are there alternatives to your product that your potential customers already know about and are heavily patronizing? What are you doing to appeal to them? How well are you solving their problems? How well do you know your customers? If you want to be successful you had better know them inside and out: their behaviors, their habits, their preferences, their patterns. How do they purchase? Online or in brick and mortar? Do they predominantly shop for discounts and sales? Do they want top-quality or are they shoppers of disposable goods or fast fashion? Are they super trendy or more classic? Are they alternative in their thinking or are they incredibly traditional?

You need to know everything about who your customer is and how your business can better serve them. You also must know what your customer expects from you and give it to them. Customers want to be loyal. Give them a reason to be. They want a relationship with your brand. Let them have one by making them feel like an insider and making them feel special. There are many ways to do this. Costco's business model is a membership-based model. Costco members are exceptionally loyal. If you are not a member then you cannot gain entry and access the amazing deals that they offer to their "family of members". Let's take it a step further in a different arena. Lady Gaga is one of the best-selling artists of all times and sells out huge arenas all over the world. She has made her fans part of her family, even referring to herself as Mother Monster and her fans are her little monsters. She has made them part of her superstar family and given them a sense of being a part of something that they will be forever loyal to because they are part of something that makes them feel connected. Another one, one that I am a part of, is the CVS loyalty club. Even though CVS is more expensive than Target and Wal-Mart, I shop at CVS because they give me great coupons, send me all kinds of sale stuff and even send me a summary of my savings and how much of a super saver I am. It will show me that I am in the top 2% of savers in California. Pretty cool, huh? This makes me want to buy more so I can be in the top 1% and maybe even be number 1 at some point. Crazy, huh? They are making me want to give them my money so I can be higher up in their club.

Make your customer part of the family that is your business and they will make your business grow. There are so many ways to do this depending on what your business is. Get creative and think outside of the box. There is no limit to how you can engage your customers and get them to sell your product or services for you.

The best way to engage customers is to solve a problem that they have. Many business owners with experience will agree that identifying the problem is often not the issue. It's probably the easiest part of it all. Designing a solution for the problem, letting people know that you have the solution, and getting them to use your solution is often the challenging part.

Let's talk about strategy. The goal of any customer knowledge strategy should be to understand the customer to the extent that this product and service fits this customer and sells itself. You will experience amazing success if you know your customers well and understand the right parameters and tools to measure success. It will also help you to develop better solutions to their problems and better understand their problems thus leading to success for your business.

One of the best ways to better understand your potential customers and existing customers is to think like an investor. What does it mean to think like an investor? Perhaps you have $100,000 to invest in a start-up business, there are certain questions you will need answers to before calling your bank. Some of those questions may look like this:

What problem are you solving?

What proof do you have that this problem exists? Who has this problem?

Why do they have this problem?

Is the problem really worth solving? How are you going to measure success?

How many people have this problem? Is this market big enough?

How much are these customers willing to pay to make this problem go away?

No serious investor will give you money if you can't answer these questions. And even if you are not at the stage where you need investors to come in, these are the questions you need to answer to ensure that you start your business with a strong foundation.

There is so much noise and competition for the attention of customers. There are only a few things that will catch a customer's attention: saving them money, making them more money, saving them time, and helping them solve their problem in a better way than anyone else has.

Every business needs a reason for customers to choose their product or service – a reason to buy from them and not their competitors. This is what is known as a Unique Sales Proposition (USP). You can identify your USP by completing this phrase: "People will patronize me because my business is the only business that..." or..." People will patronize my business because we do..... better than anyone else." If you have a wide variety of customers don't worry, your USP could be more than one. In fact, you can have different USPs for different customers.

Keep in mind that your USP may not be useful if they are mapped to a wrong customer. The more you know your customers, the more effective your sales and marketing efforts are going to be. It is worth making the effort to find out who these customers are, what they buy, and why they buy it. If you plan to sell to other businesses, then you may need to find out the individual or groups responsible for the purchasing decision and see how best you can strategize for them.

The following are the basic things you should know about your customers. This is by no means an exhaustive list but it is a good start:

Who they are.

If your product or service is sold directly to individuals, then you want to know your customer's gender, age, marital status, and job. If you are providing a business-to-business service, then you want to find out what the size and kind of business they are. Is this a small family company where anything goes or is it a corporation where there is some form of structure? Knowing the answer to this can greatly help you to design and market your product. Know your customer!

Why they buy:

If you know why your customers pay for a product or service, then it can be easier to match their needs to the benefits that your business can offer them. Know your customer!

How they buy:

Do they prefer to buy in shops or online? Do they pay cash, credit card or apps?

Do they have a high rate of returns? Know your customer.

How much they have to spend:

It will be a sheer waste of time trying to sell a $1000 dress to someone who earns $15/hr. Even though they may like it and genuinely would love to buy it, they probably can't afford it. You would have then wasted your time marketing to someone who can't afford your product. Know your customer.

What makes them feel good about their purchase?

If you are able to understand what triggers their happiness when they buy, then you can be able to serve them in the way that they will respond favorably to.

What they expect from you:

When people do business with you, there is always an expectation. Perhaps, they expect the exact product quality they saw in your catalog. Or maybe they expect you to deliver the same level of professional service you promised, there is always an expectation. They are not just paying for a product; they are paying for what they envision. Know your customer.

What they think about the competition:

If you know how your customers view competition, then you stand a good chance of staying ahead in the business. You must intimately understand your competition.

The easiest way to understand your customers and know what they want is simply by going out and talking to them. You can also offer discounts or gift with purchase if they share their opinion with you. You should ask them what product or service they use, why they use it and why they are not using others. You want to know what they may want to buy in the future and get a picture of what they find valuable.

You can drive strong sales numbers by emphasizing the benefits that your product and service offers. If you know and understand the challenges faced by your customers, then you will have a much better idea of how to sell to them.

It can be extremely important to keep yourself abreast of what is going on in the market and in the lives of your customers. Keeping yourself informed of the trends that are going to influence your customers can help you anticipate and plan for what they will need so that you can offer it to them as soon as they need it.

Look at various reputable market surveys, conduct your own research, use existing reports and build a picture of your customers' market and where you think your market is headed and you will be headed in the right direction.

CHAPTER 7

Don't Reinvent the Wheel

The road to success is always under construction

     - Lily Tomlin

What do you need to start a business? Three simple things: know your product better than anyone, know your customer, and have a burning desire to succeed.

- Dave Thomas, Founder of Wendy's

A common misconception that arises in the minds of many people when they think about entrepreneurship is that they have to do something groundbreaking or have a genius, out- of-this-world idea to be able to break through and build something substantial. Don't tell that to Toyota, or Tesla or Virgin Airlines or Marriott. There were others before them with the same type of product but that did not deter them from putting their own spin on an already existing business type or product type. Look at the market share that they have captured doing what someone else was already doing. There really is plenty to go around for everyone. There are hundreds of millions of entrepreneurs building businesses and making a good living doing things that have already been done- just doing it a little differently and doing it well.

The probability that you are going to conceive a genius idea like the invention of the computer or a drug that cures cancer is especially small. Unicorns are called unicorns because they are rare. Even if you do happen to conceive a breakthrough or groundbreaking idea, the probability that you are going to be able to turn it into a multi-billion-dollar business or a unicorn is incredibly small and that's ok. There are many businesses that are not unicorns but are very successful and lucrative.

I am not telling you this is to try and kill your spirit, it is to share the reality and set expectations and to also let you know that you are the one who determines what success is to you. It is also to encourage you to jump in and start a business. Many of us typically associate visionary leaders who have created something that none of us have seen before with entrepreneurs. This is why if you are asked to name some entrepreneurs, you will most probably name Steve Jobs, Bill Gates, Elon Musk, without even thinking about them. They are there in your memory permanently as the ultimate entrepreneurs because they changed their industries by creating things that no one in their industry has seen before and they became household names and billionaires because of it. Steve Jobs created the first computer that users can directly interface using the graphical user interface, then gifted us with the touch-screen iPhone that revolutionized the smartphone industry. Bill Gates created an Operating System that no one knew the importance of until it was made. Musk is making cars that are environmentally friendly while still being super stylish, cool and fast. By building the Tesla, Musk is not only taking on the titans of the auto industry, he also is taking on big oil and gas. Talk about challenging!

Entrepreneurial success is a wonderfully mysterious and personal thing. For me, it can be manufacturing softer, more luxurious clothing and home goods that make my customers feel cozy, comfortable and glamorous. This is nothing groundbreaking. For Mark Zuckerberg, it was creating a social network like no one had ever seen before. It was groundbreaking but no one knew the potential in the beginning except Zuckerberg himself and maybe a few who were closest to him. Imagine how many people thought he was crazy when he first started. I can just see it now. "Hey Mr. or Ms. Venture Capitalist, I created this new website that lets people connect with each other and post their vacation pictures for everyone to see. I need you to invest a million dollars so I can build it." "That's a terrible idea Mr. Zuckerberg! Everyone has a telephone and email and are already in touch with each other. Also, my mother-in-law just made us sit through a slide show of her vacation photos and it was torture. Why in the world would you think that anyone would want to see that?" Sounds silly now with Facebook being what it is today but in the beginning he was just another guy with an idea, vision and a ton of tenacity.

While it may be true that some people have blazed the trail by creating entirely new things and have become successful in the process, the statistics for that to happen to you are particularly slim, but not at all impossible. The reality for more than 95% of entrepreneurs is much different and that is OK!

Your success doesn't need to come from the creation of any earth-shattering or industry- disrupting product or service. You stand a better chance by simply making yourself open and receptive to what people need and then adjusting existing products and services to better meet the needs of your customer. If you make a product then you would be crazy not to listen to your customers. They will practically create new products for you if you pay attention and listen. They will make your products better in ways that you may have never thought of if you let them. There is a reason large companies pay tons of money for focus groups. They understand the value of feedback from their customer demographic. People will tell you exactly what they want and need, it is up to you to listen and take what you hear to make your products better.

Regardless if you are a visionary or a business that manufactures rubber bands, the game is the same. First, you need to convince people that they need what you are selling, that it addresses their concerns or solves their problem, and generally makes their life better. Then you have to overcome whatever criticism that will be thrown at your product and service (and there will be a lot), get the product or service off the ground and then continue to work to ensure that you and your company and your product stays relevant in the market and to your customers. This is a process that won't happen quickly. It often takes years for this to happen and it is a cycle that is repeated over and over again. The process of staying relevant and giving your customer what they want or need can be extremely challenging as the world is evolving at a pace much faster than it ever has before.

You don't need to reinvent the wheel. The only thing you need to do is re-imagine or put your own spin on an idea that already works. The visionaries we talked about earlier built their companies and their reputations using product innovation and changed or created entire industries, but that is not the only way to success. Assuming that this is the only path to success is ignoring the success of millions of entrepreneurs who never invented a single thing but just knew what people wanted and needed and found ways to provide these things in the way people wanted them.

I remember going to work with my dad as a child up through my teenage years until he passed away at the age of 46 years young. Every Saturday we would go around town and maintain the landscaping for a huge house on the river in Jacksonville and 6 or 7 different dry cleaners that were owned by the couple who lived in that big beautiful house on the river. Dry cleaning is nothing spectacular or innovative or even particularly creative but Mr. Johnston knew his customers and knew that they were mostly business people who needed a good price and a quick turn-around time for their dry cleaning. Sounds simple enough, right? Once he understood his customer and their needs, he was able to give them exactly what they needed. Another strategy employed by Mr. Johnston was that he strategically put his dry cleaners next to some of the largest office parks or commercial areas in Jacksonville to make it convenient for people to drop off and pick up dry cleaning. Understanding his customers like he did and executing his strategy is what made his chain of dry cleaners so successful and allowed him and his family to have the kind of life that they wanted, including that big beautiful home on the river.

There are lots and lots of products and services out there with proven demand in the market. However, many entrepreneurs pass up the opportunity to leverage these opportunities. In short, opportunities to capture and deliver value are all around us. We do not need to be blinded by the glamor that comes with reinvention. But we do need to know how to sell. To show people that you are different from what they are used to even though you are not giving them something they can wrap their heads around, you need to know how to reset their expectations.

You also need to need to know how to package your idea or business. For example, if your business is geared towards Millennials, there are ways you can humanize your brand/product and make it more appealing to that particular group, or any other group for that matter. This depends on what the product or service is. With creative packaging, you can capture the interest of your audience and give the impression of a product that is new and fresh and captures their attention. This is what will make customers want to experience your product or service.

You should never be afraid to step out into the spotlight when building your business. As one of my professors in grad school said, "You have to get out there and let people know what you have to offer. If you are the next American Idol, no one will knock on your door and ask you, 'Are you the next American Idol?'" You may need to create a lot of buzz through as many outlets as you can to let people know about your product and/or service. If you decide to market your business use taglines that are memorable, punchy and thought- provoking, you should have fewer problems getting through to your audience. Think about some of the most effective taglines of our time; Mazda's 'Zoom Zoom', FedEx's 'When it absolutely has to be there overnight' and one of the most well-known slogans is Nike's 'Just Do It'. This is easy for people to remember and it fits Nike's product offering perfectly. It can also apply to pretty much everything in your life and almost every human being can relate to it in one way or another. These companies have mastered the tagline. They all say something about the product and make you think and feel a certain way. They also make you think of the brand when you hear their tagline which translates into sales and customer loyalty.

When it comes to gaining and keeping customers, as mentioned earlier, you need to know them inside out to better understand who they are, what they want, what they want to hear, where their attention is directed, the kind of podcast they listen to, the social media platforms they visit and ensure that they see your presence in one or more areas where you can reach them and engage them.

A great way to get into the head of your customers is to approach the problem from that of your customer's point of view instead of viewing everything from your perspective. Focus on different types of entrepreneurial activities as opportunities to solve customer's problems. Get creative! That way you can build a business that can grow based on a strong foundation and can deliver outstanding value and experience to your customers on a daily basis.

CHAPTER 8

Handle Your Business

If you are under the illusion that you can start a business and run it at your life's schedule, you are mistaken. The business is like a starving puppy - when it needs to eat, then it needs to eat regardless of what you have going on personally.

- Robert Herjavec

Step out of the history that is holding you back. Step into the new story you are willing to create.

- Oprah Winfrey, media proprietor

If you take a quick sharp look at businesses over the world, whether new or old, you will find that certain qualities are common. Of course, industries may differ but essentially, businesses face the same core problems.

What are the problems? Leadership, business politics, planning, work culture, data overload, relevance, talent acquisition, production delays, labor issues, etc. We can write an entire chapter on these problems. And believe me, you will face one or more of these problems when you start. This is not meant to scare you. Entrepreneurship is about making money through problem-solving, isn't it?

The best entrepreneurs are the ones who know how to think and react their way through these problems to meet their targets and provide the very best products or services. They are the ones who understand productivity, know what is important and what isn't, and how to prioritize to maximize their time. They are the ones who can block out the 'noise' of things that are merely distractions and focus on the things that can truly make a difference. The more tasks you can do with less time, less work, and with less heart- ache, the more productive you become.

As an aspiring entrepreneur, you will find that your business doesn't care about your personal schedule. If you own a service that people pay for, people don't care about whether you want to go to the beach on a Saturday or your sister's wedding; they only know that they need you to take care of something for them. They want to know that they are getting the best service, the way they want it, and at the time they want it. I can best compare it to having a newborn baby.

I personally had this same thing happen to me and my business. I was selling blankets through a third party who is militant about her business and who expects vendors who work with her to be available to her and her customers 24/7, regardless of the day, time, holiday, etc. Our project was going very well…. until it wasn't. It was Christmas Day and I was working at the Los Angeles Mission, just like I do every Christmas Day. I did not take my cell phone in as I am working in the kitchen helping prep food and serving meals to those in need. When I left the LA Mission around 4 pm I had countless messages and emails – by countless, I mean more than 10. I called back to find out what was going on and got an earful because neither my employees nor myself had been available for what they considered an urgent matter. I was lectured about my company's lack of providing instant responses even though it was Christmas Day. This urgent matter, mind you, was a question from a customer about the washing instructions of the blanket that she had purchased. There were washing instructions on the care label but apparently that did not suffice and this was now something urgent that required my input on Christmas Day.

My employees were off enjoying the holiday with their families and I was helping out at the LA Mission. I thought this was acceptable considering it was Christmas Day. Boy was I wrong. This is why it is extremely important to create best practices and follow them when you are starting out as well as at every stage of your business. It is also equally as important to understand your customer and what their expectations are from the beginning. Had I understood my client more thoroughly I would have known that there was the possibility of receiving a phone call on Christmas Day. I will never work with this person or company again as our mission does not align with her expectations. This was an especially valuable lesson learned – and an awfully expensive one.

Creating best practices and a strong mission for your business is vital but so is having some sort of balance in your life or an outlet that allows you to clear your mind and dream. Having an outlet affects everything in your life: your health, your life/work balance, your attitude and ultimately the way you handle and build your business overall. Having balance allows you to be more productive.

Many productivity experts agree that completing three tasks before noon can give you a lot of motivation to see your day through and accomplish more. When starting your day, you may often be overwhelmed with things to do, people to call, bills to pay, orders to keep track of, investors to talk to, product modifications to make, marketers to talk to... the list is endless. Making a list of everything you need to do and prioritizing it is the most important tool you can have – and it's free! Seeing a list of what needs to get done in black and white keeps it real and keeps you from forgetting anything that you have put on the list. Sorting tasks on your list in the order of importance can help to keep you on track, stabilize your day and keep you firing on all cylinders. List makers are statistically shown to be more productive than those who do not make lists.

It may help you to break projects or goals into smaller parts or segments. If you take the shorter ones first, it can give you the motivation to power through the longer one. On the other hand, doing longer tasks first can help you get them out of the way early leaving you more time to coast through the easy ones. It may also help to do similar tasks at the same time. The mind loves repetition and you can build momentum by doing similar projects at the same time.

You will figure out what works best for you over time. Pay attention and be strategic with your decisions.

Another particularly useful business tool is called a Flash. A Flash, also called a Flash Report, is a snapshot or overview of the most important information that you need to run your business each day. The kind of information on your Flash will depend on the needs and nature of your business. It's a one- page summary of all the information you need: cash in the bank, invoices due, orders, overtime so far that week, billable hours so far that week, open orders, backlogged orders, Facebook views, website visits, leads generated, complaints to take note of. Essentially, it is a comprehensive overview of the most important information that needs to be reviewed and addressed on that particular day.

A flash ensures that you are completely abreast of the key information about your business. It shows you the key information so that you always have a pulse on your business. This is not just an exercise in how to keep account of your business but an activity that is supposed to impress on your mind the core things you are supposed to keep track and work on each day. Once you do it a few times every day, it becomes a part of you and will only take a few minutes to complete since you will already know more than half of what is on the report by heart. If you don't know these numbers by heart, then it means you are not truly running your business. If you have ever seen the TV show Shark Tank you will hear them ask about the business numbers every time. The numbers are so important and you should know them inside and out. Being immersed in the business of your business will keep these numbers clear in your mind. In addition, knowing these numbers will help you scale your business strategically. Know your numbers! Every day of every week of every year!

The Flash report should not be complex. It should be simple and straightforward. You don't need a graph or chart. Many people simply use a legal pad and manually write these numbers. You can also use an electronic spreadsheet if this works for you and have the headings already saved so that you can fill in the information more easily and quickly. There is no need to pay for expensive software. Your Gmail or Microsoft mail has a feature that let you create a memo that can be time-tracked. The point of getting a report is that you can easily see important information at a glance all in one place on one page, digest the information and act on it.

The Flash report also serves as a good way to provide some form of benchmark and comparison. How else will you know if your backlog this month is lower than last week? How do you know that you are meeting the sales forecast at the rate at which you are working if you don't document and keep yourself informed?

As a small business owner, you know that you just can't hire an accountant full-time so you have to be good at book-keeping too. It won't matter what you do, if you don't know how to keep records, your business will be in jeopardy. Therefore, using a one-page flash report can be instrumental to help you stay on track and have some form of records so you can stay on top of important happenings in your business.

In the end, how quickly your business will grow will depend on how you handle it. Do you want to handle it as something you want to do on the side as you focus your attention on more important things? Or do you consider it as something deserving of all your efforts?

Even at that, efforts can only do so much, what works is using the right strategy, then back it up by good efforts. Follow best practices in the sector you are doing business. How is your competition is dealing with delivery challenges? What is the best time to place an ad to target your customers? Are your sales reps performing? Which products are not selling? All of this is important information that your daily report should point to. It doesn't matter if they are questions or answers since your mind is impressed on it, you will find a way!

CHAPTER 9

Conviction

There are only two mistakes one can make along the road to truth; not going all the way, and not starting.

   - Buddha

Confidence comes not from always being right but from not fearing to be wrong.

- Peter T. McIntyre, Philosopher

Whenever you are starting something new; something you don't have prior experience with, the tendency to fail, the possibility to just pack up and go home is fairly high. Look at toddlers when they first start learning how to walk. They have to fall several times before they eventually know what foot to place where and how to achieve balance when walking. Running a startup is not so different at all from this. You have to make moves to achieve success. Not making that move is not an option. Your business will always be evolving or else it will be dying. Making that move comes with the possibility of failure but also the possibility of tremendous gains.

In the early stage of starting up, you will be making decisions that will ultimately shape your business as well as your personal and professional life and probably others that work with you. It is therefore very important that whatever decision you make is backed up by confidence and the understanding that even if your decision does not work out the way you want, you have a learning curve.

Starting up as an entrepreneur often requires that you make certain decisions that you have no idea would work for sure. You simply do not have all the data, money, or manpower to know for sure if an idea would work or if a decision is the right one. That's why you still have to carry out decisions with confidence even if you are not sure what the outcome will be.

Not having confidence is not a good sign for your business. At the same time, being over-confident is taking the high-road to failure. Entrepreneurs who are self-aware are those who base their confidence on their experiences no matter how small or irrelevant. In much the same way, you don't become a Grammy award-winning instrumentalist the first time you play the keyboard, so it is too with confidence. It is a muscle that becomes strengthened over practice and over time. Repetition makes it second nature. True entrepreneurial confidence is achieved from one's ability to execute in much the same way an instrumentalist is able to get self-assurance and confidence by thoroughly practicing their instrument.

Once you have built for yourself a foundation of confidence, what you want to do is strengthen your courage muscle. One way to do that is to talk to successful entrepreneurs and ask them to talk more about their failures as well as their success. Ask them a question about the decisions they made early in their careers and what decisions led them where they are now.

Once a foundation of confidence is established, the next step is to develop an appropriate level of courage. One way to enhance your bravado is to demystify entrepreneurial success. In most cases, you will find that even though they made a lot of mistakes along the way, they learned from every mistake and quickly adapted to the realities of their decisions.

Leverage on platforms like Quora, Twitter, and LinkedIn to connect with entrepreneurs and get insight into their stories. If you take good advantage of these forums, you will see that entrepreneurs rarely just happen upon success. Success happens to those who dare to remain focused on achieving success.

According to Curt Siodmark, "A man of conviction is often more desired than a man of experience. Whenever you are executing a plan, you have to do it with a lot of conviction. That is not to say you should take an uninformed decision. Your decision should be backed up by something, like data for instance. It should not just be a shoot-arrows-in-the-dark strategy. But the moment you decide to execute that strategy, you need to follow through and show commitment to that idea. By not demonstrating commitment and conviction you are creating a self-fulfilling prophecy of failure." Have a strong yet flexible conviction. Stay true to your vision but be willing and able to move and make changes at the drop of a dime.

There will be many who will try to encourage you to do things differently. There will even be some who will tell you how everything you are doing is wrong. Listen to them and think but do not be bullied into building someone else's dream and do not take their word as gospel- use it to make you think.

Always remember that your course of action or strategy should be backed up by something reliable like data. You must understand the data and what it truly shows. Misunderstanding data is as dangerous, if not more so than having no data at all. Know also that sometimes the results might not show the desired trend but having data will show you baselines and what your ideal case should be. If you are not getting the results you want as revealed by your data, then you should also try to be as flexible as possible by knowing how to respond and adapt to changes. An important key to surviving this journey is to have the courage that conviction brings but also listening to data, customers, mentor, and industry-experts in making the right decisions.

You will need to decide and act with conviction to ensure that you not only meet your major goal but also learn from mistakes and evolve. Failure is never an end; it is just a point to reassess and rethink your strategy. Failure can be your friend if you let it.

Persistence and tenacity are two of the most important characteristics a person needs to build any kind of business. You have to power through and keep going through the bumps and setbacks and challenges that will surely come your way. Being persistent doesn't mean being stuck in your ways though. It means that you keep going while being flexible enough to make changes along the way. It means not giving up because of a setback. It means staying positive and learning from each success and each failure.

Making changes along the way does not mean that you get away from your main goal, the main reason that you started this business, the problem that you're trying to fix or even the solution that you were offering. Change is good and making changes for the right reasons is true growth not just as an entrepreneur, but also as a human being.

CHAPTER 10

Giving Back

Service to others is the rent you pay for your room here on Earth.
   - Muhammad Ali.

The best way to find yourself is to lose yourself in the service of others.

- Mahatma Gandhi

The more wealth and power you get the bigger your duty becomes to help those who are less fortunate and who are suffering. Giving joyfully and helping those who are less fortunate feeds the soul.

They say, To she who much is given much is expected. This life is a lottery. You can be talented and never hit it big, you can be smart and driven and never have a billion-dollar business. I look at it this way – money and success are not happiness. Happiness comes from within. No one can give it to you or take it away from you. Money makes life more comfortable and success will give you clout and position but I know many people with millions and even billions of dollars who are extremely miserable and lonely. They are not happy and fulfilled in their heart. They have not found peace in their life. Money and power cannot give you peace or happiness or fulfillment.

One of the greatest gifts being an entrepreneur gives is the ability to help and assist other people and being able to use your business as a catalyst to do good. Being an entrepreneur gives you the platform to stretch out your hands and reach out to others. Most of us wake up every day to the hope that our lives will have more meaning than just waking up, going to work, facing challenges, and going to bed. Deep within us, we desire something more from life. When we first start out, we may need to be frugal with resources in order to make our dream a reality. This is understandable, but yet it shouldn't stop us from volunteering to help improve the lives of the people around us or in our community. Some entrepreneurs give a portion of their income to charitable organizations as a way to give back to their community and support those who support them. For others, the preference is to give their time doing something to give back or be of service to the community.

Giving back is a healthy culture to build into your life and business. When we donate or volunteer to our community where our business operates, we are directly making the community and the individuals that are members of this community much stronger and more self-sufficient. Donating and volunteering helps bring people together for a cause which could vary but is geared towards a common good. Never underestimate the power of giving back in your personal life and for your business. By organizing community events that are geared towards helping the community you serve, you are directly warming yourself and your business into the hearts of people. People may forget what you say to them but they never forget how you make them feel. Giving back makes people feel like you are strongly connected to them and you want to enrich their lives—which should be one of the main points of your business. A community of customers which is infused with charitable works can help bring hope and possibility to your life. Hope is an extremely powerful thing.

Sometimes, your daily activities as an entrepreneurial woman may start to take a toll on you and even get in the way of your focus and goals. There are many ways to clear your head and get back in focus. Exercise, meditation, taking a walk at the beach, and yes even taking time out to help others are all great ways to clear your mind and open it up for new ideas or solutions to come flooding in. Volunteering gets you out of your work space, out of the grind of the job and around other people who are inspired and giving back. Getting out helps to broaden our thinking and places us in an environment where we can make new connections, friends, and let people know what we stand for. It also gives us the opportunities to be in social situations where we can make new connections and friends and the opportunity to get involved in whatever cause we are supporting. When you get out of your own way, you open yourself up to interaction with people who run successful businesses while still placing importance on the people involved in the value chain.

You should do it for your health. How you think and feel has a clear and direct impact on your health. By volunteering and giving back to others, you can increase and strengthen your physical, emotional, and mental health. Giving back helps you to take the focus off yourself and direct your kindness towards helping others. This type of involvement fills you with a lot of love and positivity - and love heals.

Take on a leadership role when giving back. If you can find an opportunity to give back, there will almost always be an opportunity to take on a leadership role. Can this be challenging? Probably yes. But why not step outside what you are used to and try a different experience. At least, you will learn a thing or two about putting events together, working with teams, turning an idea into a crusade, and selling your idea to people of different backgrounds. It might even open up a strength or weakness you never knew you had and could open up other opportunities for you and your business. Do not put pressure on yourself to do everything perfectly. Instead, ask for help, seek passion, and donation. Be intentional about what you do. In the end, you may fumble through it but the happiness you will see on the faces of people will be your reward. Just knowing that you made someone else smile and made someone's day better could make all the difference.

There are millions of ways that you can give back. You can share your knowledge with others. Every one of us has strengths that can be used for the benefits of others. One of the best ways to use our talents, hearts, and minds is by volunteering and donating. If you are contributing to a good cause already, you will see that more can still be done. By sharing our skills and knowledge with others, we are also sharpening our skills and growing as entrepreneurs and as individuals. Active participation can make you stronger, wiser, and humbler.

Giving back can also help you stay and remain grateful. Giving new life to people and giving them hope can have a lasting effect on your life. When you give selflessly and offer support to others, the feel of appreciation and the fact that you are able to inspire hope, laughter, and happiness can help to give you humility. Contributing to the life of others has a natural effect of reaffirming your own beliefs in the importance of life, and the goodness of yourself and others.

Finally, and most importantly, you should strive to give authentically and from the heart. Let your heart drive your giving, not the need to just show- off or create some sort of facade. When you contribute in such a way that is not authentic, you are missing the point of giving completely. The universe is a system of balances. Giving without giving from the heart or giving freely and joyfully does not create balance in your life; it does not multiply the way that it does when given from the heart. People want to know that you genuinely care. It is great to share what causes you believe and are involved in, but you should do it with humility of heart. The more you give from your heart, the more meaningful your impact is – not just to others but also to yourself.

CHAPTER 11

Know Your Story and How it Ends

If I see an ending, I can work backward.
> - Arthur Miller

The most dangerous poison is the feeling of achievement. The antidote is to every evening think what can be done better tomorrow.

- Ingvar Kamprad, founder of IKEA

The personal and business goals of an entrepreneur are interwoven. Before you can set goals for your business, you have to be explicit about your personal goals and check regularly if those goals have changed or if they remain the same.

Many women want to become entrepreneurs so that they can solve a problem, build something or achieve some form of independence and control their destiny. This is a great goal but there is much more to it than that. There is often an innate need to write your own authentic story. A need to leave something behind. A need to leave a mark on an industry or a community or even leave a legacy for your family. Your story should be carefully crafted because it could be one of the many stories that inspire others for generations to come – and that is a very powerful thing.

You may start out wanting an outlet that brings out the artistic talent in people, the opportunity to use technology to better education in developing parts of the world, to empower others in some way just to mention a few. Financially, many entrepreneurs want to make quick profits, generate positive cash flow and build a company.

Some entrepreneurs simply want to build an institution that will outlive them. They may even refuse acquisition proposals regardless of the price and sell equity to employees. It is only when you can solidify your story that you can leave a legacy.

What kind of company should I build?

If you are looking to build something that can give you quick cash, then long-term sustainability will not concern you. Also, if you are more about generating money from your business so that you can afford the kind of life that you want, then you don't need to worry about creating an enterprise that will outlive you. But if you want sustainability, if you plan to build a system that you hope to sell eventually or take public, then sustainability should be very important for you and should be a part of your story.

Your personal goal should determine the size of the business you want to launch and where you want to see that business after a certain period of time. It would also address the issue of your exit strategy. If, for instance, you are seeking capital gains, then there is a need for you to build a company that is big enough to support an infrastructure that will not need your daily intervention.

What are the risks and sacrifices involved in building your vision?

If you are building a sustainable business; one whose assets will not be only you, your contact, or your skills, then it is important to know that this kind of business involves taking long-term risky bets. For example, you may need to advertise to build a brand name. You may need to pay for adverts and reinvest your profit, sell equity, or even guarantee debts personally. You may have to hire employees and trust inexperienced employees with important decisions. Also, it may take some time, often even several years before you see anything materialize.

"In the words of another entrepreneur, "When you start, you just do it, as the Nike ad says. You are naïve because you haven't made your mistakes yet. Then you learn about all the things that can go wrong. And because your equity now has value, you feel you have a lot more to lose." (HBR, https://hbr.org/1996/11/the-questions-every-entrepreneur-must-answer)

If your goal is to operate a small-scale, life-style business, you also stand to face some challenges. Talent may avoid your company since you will most likely not offer stock options and there will be limited opportunities for growth; both personal and professional. So, the long hours may never stop since no one would want to buy a company without infrastructure and a strong team. You need to start devising a long- term plan to cope with financial challenges and exit strategy from the beginning.

Entrepreneurs who want to run small businesses in which they perform all crucial tasks do not necessarily have to change their roles. In personal service companies, for example, the founders often perform client work from the moment they start the company until they retire. Transforming a growing enterprise into an entity that is capable of independent existence, however, requires the founder to take up new functions.

While forecasting and planning what the future looks like for your business, you also have to manage your business as if the company were broke. You have to build smart, utilizing available resources that will allow you to stretch your money and budgets even further. You have to inspire the people you work with to give 110% but you also have to be able to handle the firing of those who are not a good fit for the company or team and who will not be able to grow with you long term.

Many great businesses started from modest, improvised beginnings. William Hewlett and David Packard of HP fame attempted to make a bowling alley foot-fault indicator and a harmonica tuner before finally developing their first successful product, an audio oscillator. The founder of Walmart, Sam Walton started by buying a variety store in a small town in Arkansas. There are always a lot of lessons and errors in all businesses, including those that have become hugely successful today. Is it luck? Luck may play a role but it is the entrepreneur and their team who are ultimately responsible for the success.

As an entrepreneur, you must try to see things through many different sets of eyes and viewpoints. You must use your failures to do things better and use them to fuel the fire that is your passion. Failure is when you learn the most valuable lessons of all. Lasting success requires that you ask yourself the tough questions about where you want to go

CHAPTER 12

Summary and Conclusion

To reach a port, we must sail Sail, not tie at anchor
Sail, not drift.

- Franklin Roosevelt

In the absence of clearly defined goals, we become strangely loyal to performing daily acts of trivia.

- Author Unknown

Owning a business is the epitome of the American dream. It is turning your dreams and passion into reality. You will never be so proud, so frustrated, so happy, so anxious, so motivated and consumed as you are when you own a business. You must sacrifice to build your dream and to nurture it. Not everyone will understand your journey and all that you are doing to grow your business and build it into something that will ultimately become your legacy. Also, know that the foundation of America was built by entrepreneurs and small businesses. Even today, with all of the powerhouse companies, the majority of businesses are still small businesses.

You are sure to lose friends on your journey to build a business and follow your dream but that is ok. Those friends that do not support you are not worth fighting for. Your true friends will support you and stand by you while you are building your business. Keep your eye on the prize and your ultimate goals. Those who truly want the best for you will be there for you throughout your journey. You will definitely find out who your true friends are. They will cheer you on and have your back. They will understand your schedule and your challenges and will even pitch in to help at times. Keep these people close. They will be one of your greatest assets. The support and love they give you cannot be bought.

Your failures can be your friends if you learn from them. You are sure to fail more than once and make many mistakes along the way. Learn from your failures and mistakes and use them to become a better business person, a better boss, and a better human being. Strive to be a little bit better each and every day. Do not let your failures or mistakes deter you. Let them drive you and let them motivate you. They are not mistakes or failures if you learned from them – they then become valuable lessons.

Through the ups and downs always remember to enjoy the journey. The ups and downs will bring you great joy and happiness while the downs will almost crush you at times and make you consider giving it all up and going back to the cube farm (my feeble attempt at humor to describe my working for a large corporation). Remember that challenges are merely opportunities for reflection and growth. One of my favorite sayings is, "A captain does not become great by sailing in calm waters". This has served me well throughout my journey. I am strong and I will persevere... and so will you!

This is your life and the years go by so very quickly. Enjoy your journey, live your dream and go forth and prosper.

CHAPTER 13

Quick Review and Bite-Size Wisdom

- Time is your most valuable asset. Do not take it for granted. Do not waste it.
- Aggravation is the largest expense in any business. Think about it. REALLY THINK ABOUT IT.
- Run your business as if you are broke.
- The number one tool you can have is a To Do list. Make one every morning and follow it religiously. Checking items off will become a driver to your productivity. Carry over items from the day before and reprioritize as needed.
- Know your pitch and know your mission statement. Be able to share them with confidence in a moment's notice.
- Do not try to be the master of all but do try to understand all. You will be a better business person because of it.
- Find people who are experts in certain areas (web design, graphic design, digital marketing, etc.) and hire them. You cannot do it all, nor should you try to do it all.
- The more you are given the more that is asked of you.
- The more wealth, success and visibility you get the bigger your duty becomes which is to help those who have less and are suffering or in need.
- The road to success is rarely smooth and is always under construction. If it were easy everyone would do it.
- Your attitude is everything.
- How you react is entirely up to you. Different reactions will lead to different results.
- Turn every problem and challenge into a learning experience and an opportunity.
- Always have a sense of urgency. Don't put off until tomorrow what you can do today.
- Timing is everything.
- Handle your business.
- Give back. This is your duty as a human being.
- Mentor. Mentor. Mentor. There are women who will come after you. Help them and make their path easier.
- There are many paths to get to where you want to go.
- Run your business like you are broke.

- Never stop learning.
- Try to always see the bigger picture.
- A business plan should be a living document. Use it and make updates/revisions as conditions change.
- Don't get stuck in the box. Live outside of it.
- Business relationships are still relationships. We are all human. Everyone deserves to be treated with respect.
- Nurture your relationships.
- Remember the Golden Rule.
- Don't build customers, build relationships.
- Kindness wins every time. Even if you don't win
        - you still have won by being kind.
- Regardless of the behavior of others, just know that your behavior is on you and their behavior is on them. One has nothing to do with the other. Don't get sucked into someone's badness.
- Turn every cost center into a profit center.
- Honing your communication skills is a lifetime pursuit.
- Human beings are simple yet very complex creatures.
- The scariest thing that can happen to you is that your phone stops ringing.
- Do a financial checkup on yourself and your business every year. You will be amazed at how much you can save on basic services if you just ask.
- If you don't ask the answer is always no.
- Everything requires constant maintenance. You, me, your plants, your car, your business. Think about it!
- Get your business to a point where you are working proactively instead of constantly being reactive.
- It won't kill you but if it does you will be dead so you will never know that it didn't work out. The end result for all of us is death so what do you really have to lose?

Go forth and conquer!!

Xoxo,

Your cheerleader, Deanna

CHAPTER 14

Tools and Resources

There are so many tools that will help you build and run your business. Use the tools that are available to you. In order to do this, you must know what those tools are. With a little research and a few conversations with other entrepreneurs you can access a wealth of information that will help you be more organized, effective and efficient. There are so many wonderful tools that are free or inexpensive.

Make a to-do list every evening or early morning. I keep a running list so that I don't miss anything an am constantly updating my list as things come to mind or tasks and follow up items come as a result of my day to day work; it gives me a huge sense of accomplishment when I mark items off of my list. At the end of every day I look at my list with either pride of disappointment depending on how complete it is and then transfer any incomplete items to a new list. Of course, my goal is to complete the entire list every day but that is not always up to me. Oftentimes, I send an email or leave a message for something that needs to be handled and do not receive a response within the same day. This is marked as "email sent" or "message left" and will transfer over to the list for the next day until completely resolved. Your responsibility is to complete the task not just take action.

Things to do when starting out:

Handle your business.

- Business License – Do you need one? If so, get one and stay compliant. It's much easier to stay compliant than to deal with the issues that come with not being compliant.
- Permits – What permits do you need for your particular business? There are many resources that you can reference to find this information. You can call trade organizations that relate to your type of business or even call the city and/or county. People genuinely want to help most of the time.
- Resellers Permit – Are you a wholesaler or reseller? If so, you may need a resellers permit. This depends on many factors. The internet has a plethora of information to help you but please always verify what you find. Not everything on the internet is true.

- Logo – Your logo is so important to your business. Be incredibly mindful when designing your logo or having your logo designed by someone else. If you are not sure what you want it to look like and want many options without spending a ton of money you can run a contest on freelancer.com. This allows you to post a contest and get many entries that will help you see many options and hopefully find a concept that you love.

- Domain Names – Buy the domain names that are associated with you brand right away. Don't wait until later to buy the .com and .net and various variations of your brand name. All of these can be forwarded to your main domain and save you aggravation in the future when someone else potentially decides to buy related domains and cannibalize your customers.

- Website – Your website is incredibly important regardless of what your business is. As one customer said to me, "If I can not find you on the internet then you do not exist in my world." Customers want to feel like they have access to you and they want to be able to search at all hours of the day or night.

- Trademark Resources – Depending on your business, a trademark may be vital to the long-term health and success of your business. You certainly do not want to spend everything you have building a business only to be hit with a trademark infringement suit once you become successful. There are many sharks out there who watch new companies that could be related to their brand or create any type of confusion and they wait until you become successful to try to steal all of your hard work by claiming trademark infringement. If you do not have the money to defend yourself or your paperwork in order, this person can swoop in and basically take your business away.

- Freelancer – Freelancer.com is one of my favorite resources for building websites, creating logos, creating marketing materials and many other things that you may need done. Check it out. You will be happy that you did. "Freelancer. com is the world's largest freelancing and crowdsourcing marketplace by number of users and projects. We connect over 39,686,707 employers and freelancers globally from over 247 countries, regions and territories. Through our marketplace, employers can hire freelancers to do work in areas such as software development, writing, data entry and design right through to engineering, the sciences, sales and marketing, accounting and legal services." (www.freelancer. com)

- Fiverr – The Fiverr app is another favorite. They have freelancers that can do almost anything that you need done for a great price. A great resource for getting your business ready to go. "Fiverr is an online marketplace for freelance services. Founded in 2010 and based in Tel Aviv, Israel, the company provides a platform for freelancers to offer services to customers worldwide. (www.Fiverr.com)

- Vonage – Do you need a business line but don't want to pay the phone company a ridiculous amount of money for a separate phone line that may not ring that much in the beginning? Vonage is VOIP and is an inexpensive and fantastic way to get a separate business line for an incredibly reasonable rate. One of the extremely cool things about Vonage is that you can take it with you very easily if you move. Just unplug it from the old space and plug it in to your new space. That's it! It is so easy. You can also easily add features as you grow. "Vonage's VoIP phone service uses your Internet connection to make and receive calls. And with our great features, you can take your Vonage number with you on your smartphone." (www.vonage.com)

- Skype - Skype is a great way to do video calls and message contractors, vendors, clients and anyone else that you want to chat with. "Skype is a telecommunications application that specializes in providing video chat and voice calls between computers, tablets, mobile devices, the Xbox One console, and smartwatches via the Internet. Skype also provides instant messaging services. Users may transmit text, video, audio and images. Skype allows video conference calls. (www.skype.com)

- Viber – Make calls and chat internationally for free or low cost. Just download the app and you are ready to go. Viber is not available in some countries. "Viber is a calling and messaging app that connects people–no matter who they are, or where they're from. With a free and secure connection, over 1 billion users worldwide communicate with their loved ones through high-quality audio and video calls, messaging, and much more. All Viber calls and chats are protected by built-in end-to-end encryption, so you can be sure that your conversations are always secure." (www.viber.com)

- WeChat – WeChat is another way to message and chat internationally. WeChat is exceptionally popular in China and is a great way to reach your Chinese contacts for free. "WeChat is a Chinese multi-purpose messaging, social media and mobile payment app developed by Tencent. It was first released in 2011, and became one of the world's largest standalone mobile apps in 2018, with over 1 billion monthly active users. WeChat has been described as China's "app for everything" and a "super app" because of its wide range of functions." (www.wechat.com)

- WhatsApp – Chat away for free with WhatsApp. Make calls, message, and send files for free with WhatsApp. Download the app and make it easier to do business. And it's free. "WhatsApp Messenger is a freeware, cross-platform messaging and Voice over IP service owned by Facebook, Inc. It allows users to send text messages and voice messages, make voice and video calls, and share images, documents, user locations, and other media. In January 2018, WhatsApp released a standalone business app targeted at small business owners, called WhatsApp Business, to allow companies to communicate with customers who use the standard WhatsApp client." (www.whatsapp.com)

- MailChimp – Do you wonder how you can possible send out all of those emails to the people you want to reach or how you can keep all of their information safe and organized and readily available to you? MailChimp is the answer to your email campaign and contact list struggles. "Bring your audience data, marketing channels, and insights together so you can reach your goals faster. With Mailchimp, you can promote your business across email, social, landing pages, postcards, and more — all from a single platform." (www. Mailchimp.com)

- Constant Contact – Build a database of customers and send email campaigns easily and quickly with Constant Contact. At the time of this writing they even offer a 30-day money back guarantee. Try it and if you don't like it you have not wasted your money. "Constant Contact is an online marketing company offering email marketing, social media marketing, online survey, event marketing, digital storefronts, and local deals tools, primarily to small businesses, nonprofit organizations, and membership associations." (www.constantcontact.com)

- Keap – "The all-in-one CRM, sales and marketing platform for growing service businesses, because most small businesses need to start simple and grow over time. Keap is a private company that offers an e-mail marketing and sales platform for small businesses, including products to manage and optimize the customer lifecycle, customer relationship management, marketing automation, lead capture, and e-commerce. (https://keap.com)

- Upwork – "Upwork is a global freelancing platform where businesses and independent professionals connect and collaborate remotely. Upwork has twelve million registered freelancers and five million registered clients. Three million jobs are posted annually, worth a total of US$1 billion, making it the largest freelancer marketplace in the world." (www.upwork.com)

- SelfEmployed.com – "SelfEmployed.com consists a team of successful startup founders, entrepreneurs, small business owners, and freelancers. We are you. We know your opportunities, challenges, dreams and realities. While our destinations may be different, our team of entrepreneurs, freelance developers and content writers, and self-employed marketing specialists do walk in the same shoes and are on a similar journey. With our knowledge and experience, we have developed a platform, resource center, and mentoring program designed to help all current and future self-employed people around the world." (www.selfemployed.com)

- TheSelfEmployed.com – "A Web portal for all things self-employed. The site aims to be your one-stop-shop for everything you need to know to have a fun and successful entrepreneurial journey. At the site, you will find relevant articles, how-to videos, podcasts, forums, and special offers that are all designed specifically for the self-employed. But whether you use this site or not, congratulations if you too are joining the army of the self-employed. If you do it right, you are on the cusp of the new way of work, and hopefully you will have a blast." (www.TheSelfEmployed.com)

About the Author

Success is not final; failure is not fatal: it is the courage to continue that counts.

    -- Winston Churchill

The Official Version

Deanna Hodges is an entrepreneur, a dedicated business woman, humanitarian, philanthropist, a leader in the fashion industry and a coach for women. When she's not giving expert fashion advice on The Dorinda Clark Cole Show, mentoring young women and students or working on her next books, "From Victim to Victor, Turning Your Adversities Into Your Strengths and Winning at Life", "The Power of Empowering Others", "The Female Millionaire Mindset" and "Dogs of Dog Beach", this fashion executive and leadership coach spends her time networking dogs that are in kill shelters, distributing blankets, gloves, socks, scarves and other clothing to the homeless and volunteering her time at the Los Angeles Mission.

In addition, Deanna dedicates her time and resources towards planning and producing fashion events to raise awareness and money for worthy causes such as the MS Society and various dog rescues. She is also an advocate for rescue animals and supports many of Southern California's rescues and is a staunch supporter of No Kill shelters. Deanna is an avid supporter of the Los Angeles Mission and Working Wardrobes organizations, bringing support and resources to women in underserved communities and others who are less fortunate.

She holds an MBA and a Master of Arts in International Business from Webster University, both of which were earned with honors and is a member of Mensa.

The Interesting and Ugly Truth Version

So, the above is my official bio that is all nice and neat and pretty.

While all of that is true, there is so much more. Here is the full story and hopefully it will tell you more about who I really am and how I ended up here at this exact moment in time.

Everyone has a story – a path that has led them to where they are today- a series of events that have all led to the here and now. Experiences, successes, failures, good decisions and bad.

In my own words, this is my story that has put me right here right now, writing this book that I am hopeful will help you in your endeavors.

I was born in a very small town in the south. The population when I was growing up was around 2,000 people. We knew almost everyone. How could we not? My dad was born and raised in the area as were my grandparents and other generations before them.

Most of the roads in our tiny town were dirt at that time and we played in the streets as if they were one big sandbox. I did not know at the time but my family and most others around us were struggling financially and on the poorer side. My dad was working 2 jobs trying to keep us (5 kids, my mom and several dogs) afloat.

We eventually moved from this small town to an area a few towns over. My dad had managed to find a piece of land and a trailer where we would live. There were six of us and a dog in our three-bedroom 2-bathroom single wide trailer. Even though we did not have a big traditional house, my dad took great pride in our yard and making it beautiful. This was his work and his love – landscaping.

On the outside our little trailer was all dressed up by the beautiful yard my dad had landscaped over a period of several years. Our yard was landscaped entirely using surplus sod and plants from his jobs. Sometimes it was 3 pieces of sod, sometimes it was 15 and other times it was several plants. He used what he had access to and never wasted anything. The beautiful manicured yard outside hid the ugly truth of what was inside.

I grew up in an environment of abuse and mental illness. What that mental illness was I am not exactly sure. Back then no one ever diagnosed my mom's abusive and erratic behavior. They would just say, "Oh, that's just Ann. That's just how she is". And my favorite, "She's one of the meanest women we have ever met". Maybe it wasn't her fault but regardless, it had a huge impact on me, on all of us. It shaped me (good and bad) into the person that I am today.

Let me give you a few examples of the magnitude of the environment that I grew up in: I saw my mom through the years try to stab my dad, put all of his clothes in the back yard and set them on fire and even pour dirty mop water on him while he was in the bed trying to take a nap between his jobs. In one particularly memorable incident when I was maybe 4 or 5, she drove our Monte Carlo through the front of the house (our house prior to moving into the trailer) and parked it in the living room – all while we were inside. My dad was helpless when she got like this. She was so unpredictable and volatile.

The years went by and the abuse escalated. It was more targeted towards us as we got older. My mom abused me regularly for anything and everything under the sun she could think of. There were punches to my face, cuts up and down my back and legs from thin thorny switches. There were cuts from whatever she threw at me. I was removed several times by HRS (Health and Rehabilitative Services which is now called Child Protective Services) but always sent back. I was always growing stronger and more determined to get away from her.

Well, my dad died when I was a teenager – he was only 46 years old. It was one of the toughest days of my life and also one of the most transformative. The next abuse was the final one. It was then that I decided to fight back. I went to school and told my teacher that I could not dress out for gym. When she asked me why I told her that I had marks all over and everyone would be able to see them if I were in shorts and a t-shirt. I saw a look of understanding in her face. She was great. She did not make a scene or freak out. She said ok and I went about my school day without any fuss.

What happened next was one of the most humiliating things that I had ever endured at that time. I was at lunch in the lunchroom when someone from the principal's office came to get me. You could have heard a pin drop in the cafeteria. They took me to the principal's office where there were 2 police officers waiting. One was male and one was female. I was ushered into a room with the female officer and another lady from the school administration and told that I needed to take off all of my clothes so they could take pictures of the bruises, gashes, cuts and other wounds. After this I was taken downtown and officially removed from my home by HRS.

While this was a victory for me and it ended the abuse, it meant that I lost my home and my belongings as well as the little bit of security that my home had offered me, even with the abuse. I could have made any choice at this point. I lived here and there for a few years while going to school and working. I could have become a victim and followed in the footsteps of my mom, I could have just lay down and let it ruin my life or I could fight. I decided that I would fight and survive – no matter what. This has been my attitude ever since that day.

All of this and much more have made me the person I am today and have led me to write this book. One day I will write the book about my childhood and life but today is not that day.

I have forty years of work experience, thirty years in a professional capacity and have been a solo entrepreneur for approximately fifteen years. I have been through almost every challenge you can think of and I have faced obstacles I would have never dreamed of. But I have also seen the world through a much wider viewpoint and with a much stronger spirit and will. This has allowed me to survive and even be successful in this crazy, beautiful, challenging and exciting world of entrepreneurship and see things I could have never thought.

As Paul Harvey would say, "And that is the rest of the story."

Other Books by Deanna Hodges:

From Victim to Victor. Turning Your Adversities into Your Strengths and Winning at Life

Have you ever thought that your life was much harder than that of others? Have you wondered why you have been faced with so many challenges when others seem to breeze through life without much adversity? Although it may seem like you are the only one with such struggles, everyone faces major challenges of one type or another throughout their lives.

Oftentimes, these adversities can push you to do things that you may have not otherwise done and accomplish things that may not have even been on your radar prior to the event.

We have all fallen down many times and life has thrown many unpleasant things at all of us.

There is no shame in falling down as long as we get back up and show ourselves that we are resilient. Challenges will come and go and the goal is to pick ourselves up and use our challenges as motivators to go forward stronger than ever.

This book is a compilation of stories about ordinary people who have faced extraordinary adversities and thrived despite them and maybe even because of them. These stories will move you and inspire you. The people featured in this book have all picked themselves up despite challenges that would have made many of us lay down and just give up. Keep moving forward, even if it is just one baby step at a time.

Available February 2020.

The Power of Empowering Others

We all have a voice but unfortunately many women and girls do not know that they do or are afraid to use theirs. It is our job as friends and sisters and mothers and fathers and brothers and grandmothers and mentors and teachers to help empower girls and women and encourage them to find and use their voice.

Using your voice is not just about revolution or confrontation - it is about women and girls being able to be their full and complete self. It's about equality and making things right and just.

I was extremely fortunate to have a father who taught me great work ethic and to be anything I wanted to be. I was one of the fortunate ones who knew she had a voice and never thought twice about using it regardless of the consequences.

It is my hope that this book will encourage all of us (men and women) to be diligent about empowering others. It is our duty if we want a better and more equal future that gives everyone the insight and strength to find their voice and the courage to use it. There is enough for all of us. Lighting another candle only makes your light burn brighter.

Speak and Speak loudly.

Available Fall/Winter 2020

Final Thought

Twenty years from now you will be more disappointed by the things that you didn't do than by the ones you did do, so throw off the bowlines, sail away from safe harbor, catch the trade winds in your sails. Explore, Dream, Discover.

   - Mark Twain

Dream big and go out and write your own story.

I am woman…. hear me roar… and see me build!

DEANNA HODGES is a business executive, entrepreneur, speaker and business advisor. She holds an MBA and MIB from Webster University and has extensively studied adversity and the effects of mentorship on success and happiness levels.

Ms. Hodges works with clients all over the globe advising them on their business and helping them enter the US market.

She is a fashion show producer and philanthropist previously served as the fashion expert for the nationally syndicated radio program, The Dorinda Clark Cole Show.

In addition to working on books in her Woman on Top Series, speaking and managing her businesses, Ms. Hodges is a mentor to young women, an advocate for rescue animals and a committed supporter of the Los Angeles Mission and Working Wardrobes.

Her upcoming books include The Power of Empowering Others and From Victim to Victor, Tuning Your Adversities Into Your Strengths.

You can find more information about Ms. Hodges at www.deannahodges.com

Made in the USA
Lexington, KY
21 December 2019